Under Mary's Mantle

Our Lady's Love for Canada

Fr. Émile-Marie Brière

Copyright © Madonna House Publications, January 1st, 2000.
All rights reserved.

No part of this book may be reproduced, stored in a retrieval system or transmitted in any form or by any means, electronic, mechanical, or otherwise, without the written permission of Madonna House Publications.

Design by Rob Huston

Printed in Canada
First printing, January 2000

MADONNA HOUSE PUBLICATIONS
COMBERMERE • ONTARIO • CANADA • K0J 1L0

www.madonnahouse.org

Canadian Cataloguing in Publications Data

Brière, Émile
    Under Mary's mantle : Our Lady's love for Canada

ISBN 0-921440-52-9

1. Catholic Church—Canada. 2. Catholic Church—Canada—Biography. 3. Catholic Church—Canada—History. 4. Mary, Blessed Virgin, Saint. I. Title.

BX1421.2.B75 2000	282'.71	C99-901595-8

This book is set in Janson Text, designed by Nicholas Kis of Hungary in about 1690. Its strong design and clear stroke contrast combine to create text that is both elegant and easy to read. Headings are set in University Roman, from the Charleston Collection.

Table of Contents

Foreword vii
Introduction v

Questing Madonna of The New World

Early Days in New France 3
St. John Eudes and St. Louis de Montfort 15
Building on the Marian Foundations 23
On Pilgrims, Shrines, and Our Lady of the Rosary 33
Our Lady of the Cape 43
A Special Pilgrimage to Ottawa 49
Bench Marks: 1900-2000 51
The Orthodox Church and Mary 57

Mary's Love for Canada Revealed in Her Saints

St. Joseph, Husband of Mary 63

Saints of the Founding Phase

Joseph Chiwatenhwa 71
The Jesuit Martyrs 72
Blessed Catherine of St. Augustine 76
Blessed Marie of the Incarnation 78
Jeanne Mance and Ville Marie 81
Blessed Kateri Tekakwitha 85
St. Marguerite Bourgeoys 87
Jeanne LeBer 90
St. Marguerite D'Youville 92

Saints of the Nineteenth Century

Blessed Marie-Rose Durocher 99
Marcelle Mallet 102
Mother Élisabeth Bruyère 105
Élisabeth Turgeon 109
Marie-Josephte Fitzbach Roy 112
Venerable Alfred Pampalon 114
Blessed Louis-Zéphirin Moreau 118
Venerable Vital Grandin 121
Éléonore Potvin 130
Blessed Marie-Léonie Paradis 135

Saints for The New Millennium

Blessed Frédéric Jansoone 143
Blessed Dina Bélanger 149
Adolphe Chatillon 153
Gérard Raymond 156
Paul-Émile Martel 159
Bishop François-Xavier Ross 162
Father Marie-Eugène Prévost 166
Venerable Anthony Kowalczyk 170
Pauline Landry 174
Georges Vanier 177
Pauline Vanier 180
Annette Desautels 182
Catherine de Hueck Doherty 186
Cardinal Paul-Émile Léger 189
Monsignor Ralph J. Egan 192

More Canadians Who Loved Our Lady 195
Our Lady of Combermere 199

Foreword

I was 18 years old when I happened to read a book by Georges Goyeau of the French Academy entitled *The Religious Origins of Canada*. His account of the heroism and saintliness of the first settlers and missionaries from France in the 17th century was deeply moving. I realized that a country with such outstanding figures in its past had to have as part of its spiritual inheritance a tremendous potential for goodness and love.

The year was 1935, the height of the Depression, when food was rotting in farmer's fields while people starved in the cities. I asked myself who could make a difference in all this suffering, and the answer came to me: laymen and laywomen transforming the areas of politics, economics and culture.

To help bring this about I became a priest. Ordained in 1940, I threw myself into the work of fostering adult education, cooperatives, credit unions, and farmers' unions. My earnest concern was to animate and inspire lay people to build a new and better Canada.

This passion inevitably led me to Catherine Doherty, a woman of great spiritual genius, and eventually, in 1955, to the Madonna House Apostolate, founded by her. Here I discovered that Our Lady of Combermere was the guiding light and intercessor for this unique apostolic family of laymen, laywomen and priests.

Love for Our Lady and for the laity grew side by side in my heart with an enthusiasm for the great Canadians who had given their lives for the spiritual and material development of my native land.

As I studied their relationship to the Mother of God, I was struck again by a sudden flash of insight. It was 1997, and I was standing in my little log hermitage (poustinia) in

Combermere, when the thought came to me: Mary has done everything for Canada. She is truly the Mother of Canada, of the first nations as well as the francophones and anglophones and all the other cultural groups that call themselves Canadians. She is the Mother of all of us from sea to sea to sea, and she is eager to help us with all our problems. Since she is the Mother of God, she is endowed with enormous power and wisdom. We can count on her for everything. Through her we can forgive one another and be reconciled. We can move together hand in hand to create for our children an ever better place in which to be born, to grow, to thrive, to love and be loved.

Immediately I wrote to Sillery, Quebec to Sister Ghislaine Boucher, R.J.M., the moving force behind *The Marian Sources of the Canadian Church**, a remarkable collection of tracts that she had been publishing for the last 16 years. I asked for permission to use her material, and she graciously and promptly agreed, adding, "You are helping me with my work by your present project."

A further confirmation came unexpectedly one day in August 1998, when Richard and Patricia Payne attended Mass in Catherine Doherty's cabin. After Mass I mentioned to them that I was writing a book on Our Lady in Canada. I did not know then that Richard had had a distinguished career in publishing. Nor did I know that it was Our Lady who had inspired him to spearhead the well-known "Classics of Western Spirituality" put out by Paulist Press. In confirming the direction of my project he revealed that he was a Canadian in exile. Although he had been called to spend much of his working life in the United States, he and Patricia had made a lifelong study of Canada and its spiritual origins. The humble, radiant figures who shaped this nation presented themselves to his thoughts repeatedly, unfolding a vision of Canada as being in

---

* original French title = *Aux sources Mariales de l'Église Canadienne*

the heart of God's Mother. Richard's perspective goes far beyond the scope of this present work and will be published in the future as a separate book.

The greatest moments of my life have come when I stand awestruck like a little child in my poustinia marvelling at the works of God. With the appearance of *Under Mary's Mantle* and the expectation that further publications on this theme will follow, God has blessed me with another such moment.

My thanks to Msgr. Robert J. McCarthy, and the many benefactors who encouraged and supported this book.

My special thanks go out to Marg Abbott, who has faithfully transcribed all my dictations; to Mary Bazzett, who took these transcripts and gave the book its first form; to Mark Sebanc, who laboured tirelessly to bring it to press; and to Rob Huston, who saw to its cover design and final layout.

I place this book at the feet of Our Lady of Combermere, the Questing Madonna of the New World, as she leads us into the new millenium. I owe her everything. I love Canada and yearn to see us all united under our common Mother, no longer doubtful about our identity, but caring for one another and respecting one another, as we enter a new era using our gifts and charisms for God's greater glory.

In this book we mention by name some of the great people who have built this country. There are others, however, hardly less worthy, countless thousands, if not millions, whose names may be known only to God. May they all be blessed and praised!

Émile-Marie Brière,
Priest of Madonna House
Solemnity of Mary, the Mother of God, 2000

Introduction

> Were slunk, all but the wakeful nightingale;
> She all night long her amorous descant sung;
> Silence was pleas'd: now glow'd the firmament
> With living sapphires: Hesperus that led
> 'The starry host', rode brightest, till the moon,
> Rising in clouded majesty, at length
> Apparent queen unveil'd her peerless light,
> And o'er the dark her silver mantle threw.
>
> John Milton
> *Paradise Lost*, Book iv, line 598

In the bestiaries of the Middle Ages, it is the nightingale who sings of Christ's death and resurrection. It is the symbol of the soul's love, of the purest of human loves. The nightingale sings a song of a hope. A song which is simultaneously a song of sorrow and joy. From the night its melody moves from glory to Glory. Its joy cannot ignore the dark sadness of the adulterous, idolatrous loves of the day. It calls out to the shepherd for his lost sheep. Despite the fact that the male nightingale is the singer, myth makes the bird into female and calls her 'Everyman'. In the bestiaries the nightingale sings through the night under the light of the moon. She is portrayed sitting on her eggs—readying them for birth, or working busily through the night while others sleep—in order to obtain food for her children. Her song is of a mother whose child has not come, or has gone away. The nightingale lives from the belly of a paradox. For the nightingale is the Virgin Mary herself! "Hail, glorious Virgin hail... Hail, gentle nightingale!", says the bestiary. In them her light like the moon itself is drawn from the Sun. She is a silver reflection mirroring the peerless golden light of her Son. Her voice an echo of His. For Christ the Light of the World is Mary's mantle! Her song is the joyful Magnificat which heralded life at the conception of her Son. Her song is also the silent cry of lament from the foot of the Cross sung at his death. Both songs praise God and personify the ideal of every soul.

For Milton, under the nightingale queen's "silver mantle" the "peerless light" of Christ is both "unveil'd" and protected from the powers of darkness by Mary. She is the Madonna who perpetually helps us along our mysterious pathways to her Son. Under her mantle Canada was born and under it Canada's people now live. Under her mantle Canada must discover its true identity, if it is to survive as one nation. Mary of the mantle which we Catholics venerate so deeply is not just the mother of Catholics. She is the mother of All. She is our universal mother because God has made her sinless, a human person capable of loving everyone in a completely unselfish way. She is the opposite of the modern counterfeit mother, the mother of the false feminists—who consume their children or make them into inconvenient burdens. Rather she is the perfect human person, a true woman, the mother of civilization who seeks only the happiness of her children. She is everyone's spiritual mother. She seeks to fulfill her children first by giving them God's life, by nourishing them supernaturally as persons. She pours into those who call her mother a universal respect—for the awesome dignity of every soul, for the sacredness of the human family, for the wonders of all creation, for the awesome grandeur of the cosmos.

As an orthodox Roman Catholic I have learned to call her Seat of Wisdom, Spiritual Vessel, Mystical Rose, Tower of David, House of Gold, Ark of the Covenant, Morning Star and Gate of Heaven. But I have learned that people of other faiths and of no faiths have met her too. They may know her well or not very well. They will call her by different names. Through my Catholic faith I have come to know Mary as my spiritual mother—a completely caring mother, who goes in search of all her little children, especially those who have gotten themselves lost. She goes out, finds them and calls them home. I have come to discover that her children are the people of every culture, religion, race and sex. Every child of God is a child of God's mother. Some of the names may sound strange. Some may have few or no names for her, but still know something about her, even if only a little. But I know that she has cried tears of joy and sorrow with each and every one of them. She wants only to feed their hunger, care for their wounds. Like she did with her son in Nazareth, she wants to help her children grow in discovering the human possibility which each life moment offers. Spritually she sees into their womb-like potential for love. She seeks to help each one find their God-given calling, their vocation of service for others, and she helps them find themselves.

The word mantle is taken from two Latin words. From *manus* meaning hand and from *tela* meaning threads on a loom. To be under Mary's mantle is to permit our lives to be woven by Mary's weaving hands into a Godlike pattern, by the hands of the perfect handmaid of the Lord. Weaving is accomplished with such subtle, quiet movements, and with thin threads. The focus of the weaver is the meeting of warp and woof. The weaver centers on a point of convergence and encounter. Spiritually it is living in the now—between past and future. This is called a *chi rho* moment. It is a Christ moment, like Christ's life lived between an old testament past and the church future; between what was and what might be. It is constructive instead of destructive moment, if it is a moment luminous and transparent to Christ's living personal presence, a moment when we let go and let Him take over our life. When we die to self . The warp and woof threads on the loom form a Cross. At the heart of the Cross, the vertical and horizontal lines of life intersect and the weave becomes complete. It is an allegory of the eternal becoming incarnate. A moment when form and color, space and time meet and find their unity where opposites coincide but never dissolve. Such a moment holds a sacrament of opportunity. For as we live from moment to moment, invisible forms of art repeatedly emerge. They become visible virtues under wise, caring, grateful hands. They become a more or less lovely textured piece of cloth—the fabric of a life if you will : a mantle which hides, reveals and protects a divinely ordered beauty. In the words of St. Bernard of Clairvaux, "Everything comes to us through Mary."

We say that an ideal human person is someone with their head in the clouds and their feet on the ground. What kind of an earthly mantle would such a person have? Above there would be a mantle of the blue planet's heavenly atmosphere. A mantle, a delicate membrane which brings life instead of death from the fire of the Sun. Below there would be a mantle—the layer between the earth's crust and its core of fire. On such an earth would walk men whose vital organs are covered with a protective outer layer called a mantle. Such delicate mantles sustain us in life. We presuppose such mantles at our peril until the ozone layer is depleted, our immune system breaks down or the earth itself begins to shake. In his Sermon on the Nativity St. Bernard reminds us, "Suppose you were to take away the sun, which enlightens the world: what would become of the day? Take away Mary... what is left but deep obscurity, the shadow of death, pitchy blackness? Therefore it is from the depths of our hearts, from the very vitals of our being, and with all our mind and will that we must honor the Virgin Mary: for such is the will of Him who willed us to have all through Mary."

Nazareth was Mary's home with Joseph, was where Jesus spent thirty of his thirty three years. What does this say? It says the hidden family experience holds the key to human life just as the divine family is the key to eternal life. The home is where we first must discover happiness in service of each other. "Where two or three are gathered in my name I am in their midst" promised Jesus. His indwelling spirit of the love he and his Father share is the fire of love who dwells within— the Holy Spirit—whose spouse is Mary. The home fire or hearth fire has a surrounding structure called by the same sounding name 'mantel'. In the same sense it is not by chance that the incombustible mesh surrounding a Bunsen flame which produces the light by incandescence is called a mantle. Mary's mantle is Mary's mediation of the Fire of the Holy Spirit in the world. We must choose Fire or fire. Heaven or hell. If we are not to be consumed by fire or by death, we must become fire, by uniting with the fire of life, through Mary. St. Louis de Montfort was the Marian spiritual patron of both Pope John Paul II and Mother Teresa of Calcutta. Known as "the apostle of the end times" his words, filled with fiery zeal speak to us across three centuries: "How is it, then, great God, that although it is so glorious, so satisfying, so profitable to serve you, hardly anyone will support your cause?... Scarcely anyone fired with zeal for your glory will stand up and cry out, like St. Michael in the midst of his fellow angels: Quis ut Deus? Who is like God? Let me then raise the cry of alarm: "The House of God is on fire! Souls are perishing in the flames! The sanctuary itself is ablaze! Help! Help! Good people! Help our brother who is being murdered. Help our children who are being massacred. Help our kind father who is being done to death." Montfort's call is a call to the "shortest and most direct path to sanctity": through Mary. Speaking to the Holy Spirit he says "All the saints who have ever existed or will exist until the end of time, will be the outcome of your love working through Mary."

Mary the mother of God, the mother of the Church—the Body of Christ, is described by the Catholic Church's Second Vatican Council as "occupying a place in the Church which is the highest after Christ and closest to us." It is said that the best place to hide the most important things is right under our nose. The classic spiritual tale tells of the man who spends his whole life in search of the great treasure, only to return to his broken down neglected home, and discover that it was hidden there all the time, under the now rotting floor boards of his living room. Home and family are the seed of culture. Culture is taken from the Latin word *cultus* meaning worship. Our choice between the worship of the true God and the false gods of the world determines the nature of our culture. It brings us life or death as a society, as a nation, as a state.

In his book Father Émile-Marie Brière gives us a great gift. He retells Canada's story through the eyes of the many sainted souls of Canada, especially from the second nation of Canada's peoples from France, from New France and from French Canada "aflame with the idea that the new country would be Christianized through Mary." I share his conviction that spiritually every Canadian stands on the shoulders of these great sainted pioneers. Without ignoring Canadian differences Mary in her very quiet way has worked to establish within the Canadian experience to maintain the vital common ground across history, that ground of our being in the God who is Love. I am convinced that Our Lady of Combermere (the questing Madonna of Madonna House) has been prophetically active within the first, third and fourth nations which make up our beloved Canada. Mary has been more than anonymously bringing God's life to its indigenous peoples, to its English and mainly Protestant peoples, and finally to its cross cultural and inter-faith peoples—whose mainly post World War II immigration to Canada has so radically transformed the land. I believe modern Canada possesses a unique pluralistic character. It may very well play a significant role in midwifing a future theocentric world culture to replace our present banal secular, materialistic and individualistic one. This is the Holy Father's call for a culture of life to replace our present culture of death. The world must discover a freedom and democracy rooted not in a moral or religious relativism, not in a separation or denial of God's role in culture. It must discover a new pluralism, one rooted in a common acceptance of the God who is Our Father: who created heaven and earth, and who made all peoples in the divine image. Like the prodigal son of the Bible who after a life of false gods, sin, and failure returned to his Father to discover that he was the Infinite Lover, I am convinced that in our Father the Lover's House we will discover the Beloved—the Son and Love—the Holy Spirit. In our Father's House we will discover not only our own origins but the origins of the universe: nature's roots in the Tree of Life—in the tree of paradise and the tree of the Cross. In Our Father's House we will rediscover the first fruits of that Tree of Life—the dignity of the human person, the mystery of human difference which respects equality without identifying it with sameness. Here lies the fulfillment of true intimacy, of interpersonal relationship, of community, of cultural and national identity. Under this mantle, the cerebral mantle or cortex (which we Catholics touch when we say "in the name of the Father" when making the sign of the Cross) we will rediscover our bodies ordered to an authentic intellectual life, one moved under the guidance of the Holy Spirit. In Our Father's House we will discover the deepest of all freedoms, an authentic spiritual freedom which becomes embodied under the mantle of a true and eternal God, the God who is already a community of unique persons, one in the nature of living love.

I am an expatriate Canadian living in the United States. Though remaining a Canadian citizen, I have been working in Catholic communications and media since 1967, first as editor and publisher of books, and most recently as a television and film producer. But I still consider Canada my home. My formative years were spent in the parish of Our Lady of Perpetual Help, with its saintly pastor Father John O'Neill. As a young boy I was privileged to serve his daily mass under the icon of Our Lady. He was a priest of Mary. Fr. John was a magnificent preacher whose Wednesday novenas and Sunday Holy Hours were broadcast over the radio throughout the Ottawa Valley. The church was regularly so crowded that people jammed the lobby and stood on the front steps to hear his words. He shared a Marian spirituality rooted in St. Dominic and St. Bernard of Clairvaux and completed in St.

Louis Marie de Montfort's way of total consecration to Jesus through Mary. He inspired and directed for English speaking Canadians the great Marian Congress held at Ottawa's Landsdowne Park in 1947 and attended by hundreds of thousands of the faithful. As an altar boy at that event, I witnessed the Honorable Louis St. Laurent publicly and solemnly consecrate Canada to Mary's Immaculate Heart. In recent years it was like coming home to be able serve the *Missionaries of the Company of Mary*, the community St. Louis de Montfort, founded by editing and publishing in English their massive encyclopedic treatment of the spirituality of the saint, entitled *Jesus Living in Mary*. Then my son and I produced a 90 minute television docudrama on Montfort's life and another on his spirituality both for broadcast over the Catholic Global Television Network. After many years I renewed my relationship with Madonna House in 1998 during a visit over Feast of the Assumption. After attending Fr. Brière's Mass one day, he shared his work on *Under Mary's Mantle*. It was exciting! He asked me to write this introduction. That visit became another homecoming. For the connections with Madonna House had been so strong before we left Canada. The week before my wedding to Mary Patricia Ann Sheridan in 1964, was spent at Madonna House. On the eve of the wedding Catherine de Hueck Doherty gave me a gift. It was a baptismal candle which lit the baptism of each of our five children. Prior to our marriage my wife worked for Father Peter Nearing in the Canadian Bishop's Conference Social Action Department. Father Peter would become a staff priest of Madonna House that same month. Father John O'Neill, my pastor, had been chaplain of Ottawa's Friendship House founded by Catherine Doherty. All roads led to Our Lady of Combermere.

 When the publisher of Madonna House Publications sent me a copy of Fr. Brière's final manuscript, I was stunned by the image on the cover. Another sign! All roads led to Our Lady of Combermere! Prior to the 1947 Marian Congress, Fr. John and the other leaders decided that the statue of Notre

Dame du Cap would be the central image of veneration at the Congress. They decided to commission an exact replica of the original, which resides at Cap de Madeleine, which during the years following the Congress would travel from sea to sea across Canada visiting even the smallest communities. It did so under the guidance of the French Province of the Oblates of Mary Immaculate. When the statue completed its journey it was given a home in the old Oblate church of the Sacred Heart at Ottawa University. My wife and I visited her there before being wed at the English Oblate church of St. Joseph next door. When I heard that old Sacred Heart was totally consumed by fire in 1978, I assumed the statue was lost. You can imagine my surprise when I visited the new Sacred Heart Church last year and discovered the statue in a place of honor to the right of the sanctuary. The church assistant told me that the statue and a lone still burning vigil light in front of it, were the only things from the old church to survive both the great fire and the all night deluge of water poured over the rubble by the Ottawa Fire Department. Our Lady's love for Canada cannot be extinguished!

Richard J. Payne,
Feast of the Immaculate Conception, 1999

Questing Madonna of the New World

Early Days in New France, A Land of Deep Marian Roots

Deep and heart-felt devotion to Our Lady characterized the founders of Canada and its early pioneers. The Catholics of France and New France were aflame with the idea that the new country would be Christianized through Mary.

From the very earliest times Our Lady has been active as a loving Mother of her children in Canada. The first recorded miracle to be performed in this country was a rescue mission attributed to Our Lady of Roc Amadour, a title of Mary with ancient roots in France.

On his second voyage of discovery, Jacques Cartier had brought with him a picture of Our Lady of Roc Amadour. In 1536, he landed near the St. Charles River. That winter, his men began to die of scurvy. In desperate straits, he organized a pilgrimage into the woods, carrying the picture of Our Lady of Roc Amadour in procession. Attaching it to a tree, the sick sailors sang Marian hymns and implored Our Lady to heal them. Shortly afterwards, a helpful Indian told Cartier about a herbal tonic that was a cure for the scurvy. Eventually, a shrine was established on this spot.

When the fort at Quebec City was attacked and forced to surrender to the English in 1629, Samuel de Champlain, its founder, vowed to Our Lady that he would build her a chapel and promote devotion to her, if the fledgling colony was restored to French control. In 1632 his prayers were answered when a treaty gave the settlement back to France. In 1633, on his return to the colony, he made good on his promise and built a chapel that was dedicated to Our Lady of Recovery, a title of Our Lady that takes its rise from an adventure on the high seas. When a vessel had foundered, being overcome by waves, some of the crew, together with a priest aboard ship, were washed up on shore and survived. There they found a picture of Our Lady and called her Our Lady of Recovery.

The next year, in 1634, Champlain gave orders that the Angelus should be rung morning, noon, and night. Although he was a soldier and fighting man in command of a military fort, he prescribed both morning and evening prayers, as well as spiritual reading at supper.

Devotion to the Mother of Jesus continued to grow, especially in the first half of the 17th century, when the Jesuit missionaries spread devotion to the Immaculate Conception. In 1634 they established a residence at Trois-Rivières dedicated to the Immaculate Conception. Two years later, a chapel was dedicated to Our Lady under the same title. On December 8, 1635, all the Jesuits of New France placed their missionary apostolate under the protection of the Immaculate Conception of Mary, as they explained to their provincial in Paris:

"We see clearly that it must necessarily be heaven which shall convert New France... That is why we all desire to have recourse to heaven and to the most Blessed Virgin, Mother of God, through whom God is wont to work when he wishes to do that which is impossible and to convert the hearts of the most abandoned." In Huronia, St. Jean de Brébeuf trained his catechumens well, teaching them about Our Lady. Even before baptism, he had them abstain from meat on the first Saturday of the month in her honour. Referring to the children, he wrote in 1636:

"God and the Blessed Virgin be praised. These little ones from that very day when they were baptized have continued to come together every Sunday to our cabin to worship God. It was very fitting, since they had become children of

God on the day of the Immaculate Conception, that on the day of the Purification they should begin the practice of Christian devotion, to continue it for the rest of their lives, which is what we hope they will do through the intercession of the Mother of Mercy, who has shown us in no uncertain way that she wishes to be the Mother of this newborn church."*

Meanwhile, in Quebec City similar things were happening, as Father LeJeune related to his provincial in Paris:

"From the great assistance which he gives to those who honour this first dignity of the Virgin, it seems that our Lord wishes to authorize the veneration of the purity of the Immaculate Conception of his Blessed Mother. I sent to your Reverence the formulae of a vow which we made in all our residences on the 8th of December. The blessings which heaven has showered on our little labours since that time are so noticeable as to make me wish that all our Fathers of Old France, indeed of all the world, and all good souls who cherish the conversion of the people of this country would join with us in these holy vows, by offering to God all their fasts, all their prayers, all their sufferings, in honour of and thanksgiving for the Immaculate Conception of the Blessed Virgin Mary."

In the same way, in New France, the increase in the number of baptisms was credited to Our Lady's intercession, as was the spiritual growth among the new converts. For instance, a young Montagnais girl, baptized at Trois-Rivières, had shown a great devotion to the Blessed Virgin from the start. When she became seriously ill and was told she would not recover, she calmly said, "I shall go to heaven. Shall I not see the good Mary, Mother of God? And I will say to her what

---

*It might be mentioned as a matter of interest that over three hundred years later, Pope Paul VI echoed St. Jean de Brébeuf in proclaiming Mary "Mother of the Church".

I always say to her from the bottom of my heart, 'I love you, O Mother of Jesus.'"

In 1637, at Sillery, just outside Quebec City, the Jesuits hoped to establish a colony of native Christians and dedicated the first chapel to Mary Immaculate.

The feast days of Mary were celebrated with special honour by the early settlers and missionaries alike. In 1636, on December 8, it was recorded that:

"As we have chosen for patroness of the Church at Quebec the Blessed Virgin, under the title of her Conception, which we believe to have been Immaculate, at first vespers the flag was raised on a bastion of the fort and a salute of cannons fired. In the morning at sunrise the artillery with a salvo of guns again expressed our joy. The inhabitants themselves, in testimony of their devotion to the Blessed Virgin and of their belief in her purity from the time of her conception, fired a volley from whatever firearms they had and many received Holy Communion in her honour."

On the first day of the following May the Governor had a large flag pole erected in front of the chapel of Our Lady of Recovery. It was surmounted by a triple crown. Half way up, one above the other, were three circular shields, decorated with garlands and bearing on them three beautiful names—Jesus, Mary, Joseph—written as though on an escutcheon. A squad of the artillery stood as guards of honour and fired a salute.

Meanwhile, during the same month of May, 1637, at the Jesuit mission in Huronia, in the village of Ossossane, a residence was being built, dedicated to the Immaculate Conception. When it was completed, Father Pierre Pijart, a priest at the mission, wrote that, "On the 5th day of this month in June, I celebrated the first Mass in our house of the Conception of Our Lady, saying a votive Mass of the Blessed Trinity. The next day I said the Mass of the Immaculate

Conception, invoking our Lady as a particular patroness of this new dwelling."

Soon afterwards, at the same village, a virulent epidemic broke out with the coming of the Jesuit missionaries. Although the chiefs attributed this pestilence to them, it came as a great surprise that they did not kill them. The priests felt that their deliverance was due to the Most Blessed Virgin. On this occasion they vowed to say a novena of Masses in honour of the Immaculate Conception. Accordingly, they prayed to Our Lady and many different native people came to be baptized. A celebrated Jesuit of the times, Father Jerome Lalemant, wrote:

"We seemed to have reason for recognizing and celebrating this holy day, dedicated to the first privilege of the Blessed Virgin, as the birthday of this young church and of the happiness and blessing of this country. We certainly have reason to believe that she, in whose honour this feast of the Immaculate Conception is celebrated, put her hand to the work and that it is she who has brought it to the stage which we, with a consolation which cannot be expressed, now witness."

In 1639 the Jesuits decided to establish a central station for their missions in Huronia on the shores of Georgian Bay, calling it Sainte Marie Among the Hurons in honour of Our Lady. This became the focal point of a vibrant, young Christian community, where 20 Jesuit priests and 40 lay missionaries laboured to bring Christ to the native people. It had a church, a hospital, a school, and a residence for the missionaries. The first sodality of Our Lady on Canadian soil was established here. By 1648 about 10,000 Hurons had been baptized in the areas around the Great Lakes. Between the years 1648 and 1651, however, this thriving mission was destroyed by the Iroquois, and many Jesuits were martyred, among them Jean de Brébeuf and his companions.

In 1639 the very first missionary women in the history of the Catholic Church were sent to Canada. These first women missionaries arrived in two groups in Quebec City, accompanied by a few lay women. The first trio, led by Blessed Marie of the Incarnation, were Ursuline nuns. The second three were Hôtel-Dieu nuns, nurses known as Hospitallers.

At Christmas, in 1633, while still in France, Blessed Marie of the Incarnation had experienced a dream vision in which she was shown Our Lady holding the Child Jesus in her arms above a little church that overlooked a vast country of plains and mountains. In this symbolic way Our Lady proclaimed two Marian dogmas: Mary as Mother of God and Mary as Mother of the Church. Blessed Marie was devoted to the Blessed Trinity, the Sacred Heart of Jesus, and the Sacred Heart of Mary. Each night she ended the day with this prayer:

"O my divine spouse. What shall I render you for the excess of your love for me? It is through your divine Mother that I wish to offer you my thanksgivings. I present to you her Sacred Heart, just as I present yours to your Father. I love you by that Sacred Heart which has so loved you."

At this time, the aspect of Mary's Sacred or Immaculate Heart had become very popular in France, especially in Normandy owing to the zeal of St. John Eudes. There is a beautiful phrase from St. Augustine that could be said to be the touchstone of this devotion: "Mary conceived Jesus in her heart before she carried him in her womb."

Blessed Catherine of St. Augustine, a victim soul who has been called co-foundress of the Canadian Church, arrived in Quebec City in 1648 as a nun and a nurse. Although she was only 16 years old, she also had a great attachment to the Sacred Heart of Mary, having made a retreat under the direction of St. John Eudes. She spread this devotion, especially when she became her order's mistress of novices. Later on, her pupils did likewise.

The new colony that had become home to Blessed Marie and Blessed Catherine harboured a great devotion to Our Lady. In 1657 the first men's Marian sodality was established in Quebec with 12 members. Every Saturday, in her honour, the colonists attended Mass, listened to a Marian sermon, and received the sacraments. The results were splendid. Newlyweds, for example, would consecrate their vows to the holy Virgin. Families said their morning and night prayers. The people grew in the virtue of purity. Like the first Christians, they made a great effort to live in a spirit of fraternal charity.

Father Pierre-Joseph Chaumonot, S.J., also a missionary to New France, wrote this deeply-felt request to St. John Eudes:

"I was consoled to hear of your holy ambition of loving Our Lady more than anybody else. May you communicate this gift to all the ambitious people of the world. I dare ask you, for the love of Mary, Virgin Mother, whom you love so much, to give me the grace of being accepted as the last one of her servants to her service. Should you die before me, would you leave me as a heritage, as much as you can, a part of the devotion you have for her so that you may continue, even after your death, to honour her on earth, in my person."

In 1659 Blessed François de Montmorency Laval arrived in Quebec City, having been consecrated on December 8 of the previous year in Paris as its first bishop, the first vicar apostolic to New France. As a young priest he had been formed by teachers who were strongly influenced by devotion to the Sacred Heart of Mary as preached by St. John Eudes. Indeed, he was an intimate friend of this Marian saint. As well, he was a great promoter of veneration for the Holy Family and could truly be said to be a pioneer of this devotion for the universal Church.

Every year Bishop Laval celebrated a Mass in honour of the Sacred Heart of Mary. On December 23, 1662, it was he who gave the Imprimatur to St. John Eudes' book, *The Admirable Heart of the Mother of God*, and endorsed it:

"We do not merely pretend to approve of this book, but we desire to witness publicly to our appreciation and the desire that we have that the devotion this book teaches be profoundly engraved in the hearts of Christians and that the Feasts and Offices and Masses contained in this book be celebrated with proper solemnity and piety."

On July 11, 1666, Bishop Laval took a further step in honouring Our Lady. He solemnly consecrated his cathedral, the mother basilica of North America, to the Immaculate Conception. At length, in 1686, he was succeeded by Bishop Jean-Baptiste de Saint-Vallier, also devoted to Our Lady.

In 1690 Sir William Phips, the governor of Massachusetts, attacked Quebec but was defeated by the French governor, the comte de Frontenac. The people, who had stormed heaven with their prayers, attributed this unexpected deliverance to Our Lady. Her picture was carried in triumph, and the new church in Lower Town, which is still in existence, was dedicated to her under the title of Our Lady of Victory. The whole country was confirmed once more as the land of Our Lady. Then again in 1711 Our Lady protected the colony, when a large English flotilla under the command of Sir Hovenden Walker came to attack Quebec, but was shipwrecked on the shores of Egg Island in the Gulf of Saint Lawrence.

Besides Quebec City, the other burgeoning settlement in New France was Montreal. The story of its founding is an awe-inspiring epic of evangelization and devotion to Our Lady. This great city was founded in 1642 by zealous lay apostles and named *Ville-Marie de Montréal*, "Mary's City of Montreal", destined to produce many saints. The glorious fact that it was predominantly lay people who were involved in this venture must be stressed. The main organizing force behind the foundation and support of this new town was in fact a group that called itself the Company of Our Lady of Montreal, which was composed of quite prominent Christians, mostly lay people, who guided the enterprise from afar in France. Two of its principal leaders, Jean-Jacques Olier and Jerome le Royer, Sieur de la Dauversière, were outstanding men of God.

Olier was a holy priest, the founder of the priestly Society of Saint Sulpice, whose members he sent to Ville Marie on his deathbed in 1657. The Mary-inspired Sulpicians whom he sent to the new settlement were to become its spiritual mainstay for generations to come. They took over the original parish church in Montreal, which is dedicated quite simply to Our Lady and is now the glorious basilica of Notre Dame attracting pilgrims from around the world.

As for Jerome le Royer, a husband and father of five children, he was consecrated to Our Lady early in life. Through her inspiration, he, a layman, founded the Congregation of the Daughters Hospitallers of St. Joseph around 1635 and went on to help establish the Company of Our Lady of Montreal.

The leaders of the group that actually landed at the present-day site of Montreal were Jeanne Mance and Paul Chomedy, Sieur de Maisonneuve, both of them being lay Christians as well. Together with 50 soldiers and settlers, they arrived on an island some 160 miles upstream from Quebec City, which they promptly consecrated to Our Lady. As soon as their boats reached the island of Montreal, an altar was set up, so that Mass could be offered. Jeanne Mance collected fireflies in a bottle to use as vigil lights.

Soon afterwards, a lay Marian community was established in Ville Marie, made up of five men and five women, who tried to live as the first Christians did, sharing everything. In 1652, when the town was threatened by the Iroquois, the soldiers put themselves under the protection of Our Lady, who saved the settlement. Similarly, in the town of Trois-

Rivières, which was threatened by the Iroquois between the years 1650 and 1653, the families established little oratories to Our Lady in their homes, where people would gather nightly to pray for their deliverance. Peace was made with the Iroquois in 1654.

The year 1653 saw the arrival of St. Marguerite Bourgeoys in Ville Marie from France. She brought with her a tremendous love for Our Lady, who had told her: "Go without fear. I shall be with you." In New France, St. Marguerite founded the sisters of the Congregation of Notre Dame, named after Our Lady, and had a still-famous chapel built, dedicating it to Our Lady of Good Help. This saint did much to foster courage, faith, and spiritual enthusiasm among the girls and older women of the colony.

For the early settlers of New France, their attachment to Our Lady blossomed outwards to include a special veneration for her mother, St. Anne. From the very first, the Jesuit and Récollet missionaries were keen on spreading devotion to her. The beginnings of her great shrine at St. Anne de Beaupré, 20 miles east of Quebec City, on the St. Lawrence River, were established in 1658, when some Breton sailors were saved from shipwreck by her intervention and set up a small chapel in her honour there. A scant seven years later, in 1665, Blessed Marie of the Incarnation wrote to her son about it in glowing terms:

"Seven leagues from here, there is a church of St. Anne, in which the Lord works great wonders in favour of the holy mother of the Most Holy Virgin. There one can see paralytics walk, blind people see and the sick, whatever may be their malady, recover their health."

Since those early days, tens of millions of pilgrims have visited this holy place, paying homage to the grandmother of Jesus.

In the 17th century, as well, the foundations of Canada's national shrine to Our Lady of the Cape, as she is called, were laid at Cap-de-la-Madeleine, Quebec, near Trois-Rivières. The first shrine to Our Lady, a wooden chapel, was erected there in 1659, a new stone sanctuary taking its place in 1714 by order of Bishop Saint-Vallier.

By praying to Our Lady and honouring her in all these ways the young Canadian nation was putting down deep Marian roots that would give it the anchoring strength to weather life's spiritual storms for centuries to come. The fervent devotion of Canada's earliest pioneers to their Mother in heaven was to yield a glorious harvest of saints and holy people down through the ages.

St. John Eudes and St. Louis-Marie de Montfort
The Lasting Influence of Two Great Marian Saints

St. John Eudes is famous for having spread devotion to the Sacred Hearts of Jesus and Mary, which had a great effect on the development of Marian spirituality in Canada right from its earliest days in New France. St. Louis-Marie de Montfort came a generation later than St. John Eudes. His concept of true devotion to Our Lady has played a very significant role in the Church, especially in modern times. Our own foundress, Catherine Doherty, was deeply influenced by his approach, as is our Holy Father, John Paul II.

Turning first to St. John Eudes, I feel I have a personal relationship with this saint, inasmuch as my ancestor, Jean Brière, was from Lisieux, and St. John certainly did preach there before Jean Brière left for Canada. No doubt many of the first settlers of Canada heard St. John Eudes preach as well, carrying this devotion with them to their new home.

St. John Eudes was a Norman, born in Caen in 1601. As a priest, he preached parish missions and recognized the great need for priests to have good training and formation. The Society of Jesus and Mary was the institute he founded for this purpose, and to this day it conducts seminaries, colleges, and schools. He also founded the Congregation of Our Lady of Charity of the Refuge to help women of ill-repute. During the 19th century this Congregation divided into two groups, Our Lady of Charity of the Refuge and Our Lady of Charity of the Good Shepherd of Angers. In addition to this, he established the Society of the Heart of the Mother Most Admirable, which resembles the third orders of St. Francis and St. Dominic.

During the 60 some years that St. John Eudes travelled to the villages and towns of France, especially those of Normandy, to preach his extraordinary parish missions, he would come to a given parish with a band of devoted helpers, who very seldom numbered fewer than 12 and often 30 and more. The missions lasted at least six weeks, sometimes longer. His mission in Rennes in 1670, for example, lasted nearly five months.

Besides the sermons given to all in general, the missionaries taught catechism to the little ones to prepare them for First Communion. They would give special conferences to the nobility, to workmen, to priests and even to religious. In the evenings they visited families in their homes to say night prayers with them. Leagues would be formed against blasphemy and dueling. Nearly always during the mission they organized a pilgrimage to some neighbouring sanctuary, and the exercises usually ended with a procession in honour of the Blessed Sacrament.

Missions so powerfully organized and conducted with such zeal could not fail to yield marvellous results. Sometimes whole cities were regenerated. The people pressed around the confessionals in crowds, and the missionaries often had the sorrow of not being able to hear all who came.

St. John Eudes brought true spiritual renewal to the province of Normandy. He also became the apostle of devotion to the Sacred Hearts of Jesus and Mary, a devotion not well known before his time. It must be remembered that this occurred before Our Lord's apparitions to St. Margaret Mary Alacoque. St. John Eudes was the first to organize this devotion and make it popular. He dedicated his Congregation of Our Lady of Charity to the Sacred Heart of Mary and he would often remind his daughters of the honour which was theirs.

He also dedicated the Society of Jesus and Mary to the Heart of Jesus and that of his Holy Mother. Composing prayers to their Sacred Hearts, he conceived the idea of celebrating solemn liturgical feasts in their honour. The first of these feasts to see the light of day was that of the Heart of Mary, which was celebrated on February 8 and was made the patronal feast of his institutes. It was St. John Eudes himself who composed the Mass and Office proper to the feast and endeavored to propagate it among the faithful. This liturgical feast made its first appearance in 1648, and several bishops approved of it. In 1672 he wrote a Mass and an office for a feast of the Sacred Heart of Jesus. This too was adopted by several dioceses and communities. In the decree of his beatification, Pope St. Pius X called him the father, doctor and apostle of devotion to the Sacred Hearts.

In 1673, Our Lord revealed to St. Margaret Mary the secrets of his Heart and shortly afterwards, in 1675, he asked her to institute in his honour the Feast of Reparation, the date of which he fixed as the Friday following the Octave of Corpus Christi. This feast is still celebrated in our time. Father Eudes died in 1680, before the message of these revelations to St. Margaret Mary had spread. Even so, he had certainly prepared the way for her.

Concerning the heart of Mary, St. John Eudes wrote, "Abide in the motherly heart of your dear mother. It is one with the divine heart of her son Jesus. Let it be the place of your rest."

St. Louis-Marie Grignion was born in the Brittany town of Montfort, France in 1673, just seven years before the death of St. John Eudes. Later Louis Marie would drop his family name and take that of Montfort, because it was there that he was baptized into God's life—becoming a child of God.

Educated at St. Sulpice in Paris, he became a priest and was commissioned by the Holy Father to be his 'apostolic missionary' to the local churches of France. He preached parish missions especially in the Vendée region of Western France. Possessed of great humility, he had a profound love for the poor. He became Our Lady's missionary of 'God Alone', living by Divine Providence; he owned only his ragged clothes, bible and handmade rosary. A troubadour, artist of God's love he walked the French countryside bringing his simple, ordinary 'beloved lay people' to Jesus through Mary. He wrote many remarkable works including, *True Devotion to the Blessed Virgin* and *Love of Eternal Wisdom*. Three religious congregations originate from him. First, *The Daughters of Wisdom*, whose first Superior was Blessed Marie Louise Trichet. He yearned intensely for a company of vagabond preachers, inflamed by the Holy Spirit, united with Mary His Spouse and thus totally abandoned to God. This order of priests became known as *The Missionaries of the Company of Mary (The Montfort Missionaries)*. St. Louis-Marie begged God to send missionaries to his community who would be "as free as the clouds that sail high above the earth... but in bondage to your love and your will. Men who will range far and wide with the Gospel pouring from their lips like a bright and burning flame. With the Rosary in their hands, baying like watchdogs, burning like fire, dispelling the darkness of the world. Lighting it up like the sun." Third we have the Brothers of St. Gabriel, a teaching community whose schools throughout the world would become models of Catholic education.

In his lifetime, St. Louis-Marie had a great influence which caused him to be both loved and hated. Several times attempts were made on his life. He lived in the days of high Jansenism, and his constant proclamation of God's love angered the dour proponents of this heresy.

St. Louis-Marie died in 1716 after only sixteen years as a priest. The manuscript of *True Devotion to the Blessed Virgin* which he prophesied would be lost was, only to be rediscovered and published for the first time in 1842. Since then this classic has initiated a worldwide movement of renewal of the Church through Mary. Beatified in 1888 and canonized in 1947 Pope Pius XII praised his teachings greatly. Mother Teresa of Calcutta chose him as a spiritual patron for her community. Pope John Paul II, who stated that his encounter with Montfort spirituality was "the decisive turning point" in his life, chose for his episcopal motto Montfort's short formula of consecration, "Totus Tuus", which means "totally yours" in Latin.

Today there is a worldwide movement seeking to have Montfort become a Doctor of the Church and patron of the new evangelization. For Louis-Marie appears to capture the spirit and hunger of our own time in a uniquely inspired way. The saint was utterly convinced that the world had no future without surrender to God's life, to an unselfish love and service beyond worldly self centeredness. Mary was his secret and "most direct way", the ideal human person, the personal guide through Incarnate Wisdom into the mysterious depths of the Trinitarian life.

Here is a sampling of some of the key terms he used to illustrate his beliefs:

1. *Consecration:* Sometimes used as a kind of umbrella term describing Montfort's complete doctrine, it reflects the explicit giving of oneself to God. It is a an outer expression of an inner expression of a true devotion to Our Lady for it signifies a resolve to live for her Son according to her maternal care: "Consecration of oneself to Jesus Christ, Wisdom Incarnate, by the hands of Mary". This devotion is also called "perfect renewal of baptism"—an adult renewal of one's infant baptismal promises. Montfort's parish missions were a Eucharist-centered preparation for the people freely choosing to sign a "covenant agreement"—a renewed commitment to live out their baptismal promises.

2. *Marian:* Montfort's Marian teaching can only be grasped by understanding the keystone of all his doctrine: the principle of God Alone. For Montfort this God is a Trinity of Sacred Persons, one in Love. Infinite Love is only effectively answered by Jesus' redemptive cry of love from the Cross. Central for Montfort is Mary's "yes" at the Annunciation and her accepting to become our mother to behold at the Cross. She is the summary of the Church's complete acceptance of Jesus, harmony and unity with Jesus, acceptance of Jesus and receptivity to Jesus and thus to the life of the Holy Trinity.

3. *Trinitarian:* Montfort's Trinitarian teaching is essentially pastoral rather than dogmatic. He places it at the heart of his missionary endeavors and at the heart of every Christian's practical calling. It highlights the dignity of every person, who is made in the image and likeness of God, who is more than an individual: who is essentially a relational person—a person of community, charity and love. A person whose nature is human but whose true life is drawn from a supernatural, transcendent source. In this sense, for Montfort Mary is "the echo of God"—as "daughter of God the Father, mother of God the Son and spouse of the Holy Spirit".

4. *Mold:* In Montfort spirituality the Mother of Jesus Christ, who is the Mother of the Church, is thus the womb which begets our spiritual life and growth. She is our spirituality. She molds us into Christlike persons, into living images of God. She is the mother of the most basic, the most fundamental mystery of Christianity—that of the Incarnation. For she is the mother of the one true God who becomes flesh and dwells among us until the end of time and beyond. She is our true mother, through whom we obtain God's life in the sacrament of each and every life moment

on earth, and God's infinite and eternal life of happiness lived face to face with the Lord forever in heaven.

Montfort plays a providential role as an instrument of the Light of the World. He shows us the true light of an ageless enlightenment and the centrality of Mary's role in bringing us to that Light in history. Montfort's light was Jesus— the person of Incarnate Wisdom. Montfort's Resurrected Light comes to us only through the victory of the Cross—"the true act of Wisdom"—the mission of the God who is unselfish love. The mission of "a slave" to Ultimate Freedom who came to offer us the ultimate free choice—that of choosing either the abundant life he offers, or imprisonment in other than God; a cell of eternal isolation. Montfort offers to all a mission of silent and quiet receptivity to God—a life lived for who is "other"; A hidden life which goes generally unnoticed in our overt, violent, aggressive and controlling self-centered world. He summarizes Mary's past, present, and future role in these words from *Love of Eternal Wisdom*:

"When the time appointed for the redemption of mankind had come, Eternal Wisdom built himself a house worthy to be his dwelling-place. He created the Holy Virgin, forming her in the womb of St. Anne with even greater delight than he had derived from creating the universe... The torrential outpouring of God's infinite goodness, which had been rudely stemmed by the sins of men since the beginning of the world, was now released precipitately and in full flood into the heart of Mary. Eternal Wisdom gave to her all the graces which Adam and all his descendants would have received so liberally from him had they remained in their original state of justice. The fullness of God... was poured into Mary insofar as a creature is capable of receiving it."

Building on the Marian Foundations

Jean-Baptiste de Saint-Vallier came here first as Bishop Laval's vicar general, then returned to France a year later in 1686 to be consecrated the second Bishop of New France. Bishop Saint-Vallier was to lead the young Church for a period of forty-two years. During this time, it was he who consolidated the gains of the first founders, setting them on a stable footing.

He did this by strengthening two basic institutions: the family and the parish. By his efforts, the Rosary became a normal family prayer. Under his capable direction, parishes were established where authentic Catholic doctrine was taught, including devotion to Mary. In the main he accomplished his work of instruction by writing both a *Catechism* and a *Ritual* for New France.

His *Catechism*, which appeared in 1702, was a real bulwark of the Catholic Faith and was used extensively in home, church, and school. Divided into three parts, it covered Bible stories, Christian doctrine, and feasts of the Church. Under this last heading, we find lessons dealing with the following Marian feasts: the Immaculate Conception, the Holy Family, the Purification, the Annunciation, the Visitation, the Assumption, the Nativity, the Presentation, the Holy Name of Mary, the Holy Rosary, and Our Lady of Victory.

His *Ritual*, which came out the following year, gave due emphasis to the celebration of the feasts of the Immaculate Conception, the Purification, the Annunciation, the Assumption, the Nativity of Mary, and Our Lady of Victory.

On March 7, 1701, at the end of a letter to his priests about their parishioners, he wrote:

"You will remember to continue to establish them and support them in the practice of a solid devotion to the Holy Virgin. Under the care of so powerful and tender a protectress they will have nothing to fear."

Like Bishop Laval, his saintly predecessor, Bishop Saint-Vallier promoted devotion to the holy heart of Mary and encouraged recitation of the Rosary. Immediately after the British were defeated in 1690, he established the liturgical feast of Our Lady of Victory, to acknowledge her help.

A great wave of enthusiasm for Our Lady swept through the country, and as a result a liturgical feast of the Holy Heart of Mary was celebrated everywhere with a Mass, "to honour", as Bishop Saint-Vallier said, "this most Holy Heart, Seat of Love and Charity, full of holiness, channel of all the blessings which flow from heaven to earth." On January 1, 1722, he instituted a Confraternity of the Heart of Mary in the parish church of Montreal.

Bishop Saint-Vallier had asked the Hospitallers of the Hôtel-Dieu to found a general hospital in Quebec City. Shortly afterwards, he established a chapel there, dedicated to the Heart of Mary. Consecrating it himself with great solemnity, he had a painting placed there which showed him kneeling before the Heart of Heaven's Queen. Until his death, he prayed there five hours each day.

In order that his people might turn to Mary in all their difficulties, Bishop Saint-Vallier stressed her power of intercession, protecting and guiding them. He encouraged them to contemplate Mary's life and virtues, in order to imitate her in their own daily pursuits.

Through his *Catechism* and *Ritual* in particular, he had a significant effect on the spiritual development of the colony, not only during the years that he shepherded his flock, but for some two centuries afterwards.

Thanks to him and to the early founders of the Church in New France, Marian devotion flourished in the new world, giving the people the spiritual strength to survive the political storms that were brewing. From 1755 onwards, as the British began their conquest of the country, the people prayed fervently for Mary's protection during a time of upheaval.

After the finalization of the British conquest in 1763, the Church had to fight for its survival. For some years there was a decline of religious fervour, but this was soon remedied by the advent of the greatest Canadian bishop of the 19th century, Ignatius Bourget, who led the Church of Montreal from 1840 to 1896.

This strong leader was born in the parish of St. Joseph of Lévis, on October 30, 1799, the eleventh child in a farm family of 13. In 1811 he entered the junior seminary of Quebec and a year later became a member of the Congregation of the Blessed Virgin. There the Marian formation he had already received in his family was strengthened and included: daily prayers in honour of Mary Immaculate, celebration of the Little Office of her Conception, and the Rosary.

A year after his ordination as a priest on November 30, 1822, he became rector of the flourishing seminary. For 10 years he was intimately associated with Bishop Jacques Lartigue, helping him address the problems of the diocese.

At length, the Diocese of Montreal was erected as a separate entity on May 13, 1836. Bishop Lartigue, who was named the first bishop of this new diocese, immediately appointed two vicars general: Father Bourget and Father Joseph Vincent Quiblier. On May 15, 1837, at the age of 38, Father Bourget was elected bishop co-adjutor of Bishop Lartigue. Immediately he devoted himself to all the pastoral tasks proper to a bishop.

On April 3, 1840, Bishop Lartigue died, and that same day Bishop Bourget became the second Bishop of Montreal. Immediately, he placed himself and the diocese under the protection of the Mother of God, as his predecessor had done, reminding his people that they belonged to Mary, their patroness and protector. "How could we not love a city, which is the object of Mary's maternal affection" he said, "a city which under the glorious name of Mary was built on the solid foundations of the founders' piety towards the Queen of the Universe, a city which contains so many precious monuments dedicated to Mary, a city which counts among its people, so many souls devoted to Mary?"

Often in his pastoral letters he refers to Our Lady, as, for example, in this letter of January 6, 1850:

"O Mary, Mother of this Diocese that you love so much, do not abandon it to our weakness and inexperience. Otherwise, it will be lost. During the stormy times, as we ride a sea battered by hostile waves, be our Star and guide us to the Port."

To spread Marian piety and devotion, Bishop Bourget established several organizations. The first was the Archconfraternity of the Most Holy and Immaculate Heart of Mary, which he introduced in 1841. Following the example of the first bishops of the Church in New France, Bishop Bourget desired to promote this devotion, convinced that: "Rivers of living waters coming from the throne of God, passing through the heart of Mary, would fertilize all the areas of this vast diocese."

Bishop Bourget was firm in maintaining that Mary always leads to Jesus. "We cannot separate in our love these hearts which divine wisdom has so intimately united. Let us go to the Heart of Jesus through the Heart of Mary," he maintained.

In 1847, he revived devotion to Our Lady of Good Help. Her statue had resided in a chapel that burned down in 1754, after which a second chapel was built. In 1831, however, her statue was stolen, and devotion to Our Lady of Good Help reached a new low. Nevertheless, the bishop, for his part, made a vow to re-establish the pilgrimage to Our Lady under this title. In the chapel there he initiated the Confraternity of Our Lady Help of Christians, so as to "destroy the terrible vices of drunkenness and impurity which ruin bodies and souls, to our great unhappiness in time and in eternity."

On May 21, 1848, he solemnly blessed and crowned a new statue, which was carried in procession in the middle of a great throng of people and then placed with respect in a highly visible place in the chapel so that, when they saw the humble Virgin of Nazareth, all might be reminded that she reigns as queen over the city and diocese. "There she is standing full of love, to rush to our help, her eyes filled with the graces of mercy," he explained to his flock.

On December 8, 1854, Pope Pius IX proclaimed as a dogma that the Blessed Virgin Mary was conceived immaculate and completely preserved from all stain of original sin. Bishop Bourget was present in Rome at this momentous ceremony, comparing his joy on the occasion to the happiness of heaven. To his priests, he wrote on March 10, 1858:

"Now more than ever the Dogma of the Immaculate Conception is like the sun which must dissipate the fog of errors which agitate the spirit of nations."

Again, later, he wrote to encourage and direct his people: "Every night recite the Rosary as a family to obtain from the Immaculate Virgin Mary a share in her incomparable purity."

This admirable bishop also fostered devotion to Our Lady of Sorrows, the title which honours Mary in the sorrows that she endured while accompanying her Son in his work of redemption.

During Bishop Bourget's time, Mother Émilie Gamelin of Montreal turned to Mary in her own sorrows, after she had lost her husband and last son. Mary granted her a great compassion for elderly and sick women. As a result, she founded the Sisters of Providence under the direction and approval of

Bishop Bourget, who asked the Sisters "to spread devotion to Our Lady of Sorrows... ."

He himself joined the Third Order of the Servites of Mary, on July 7, 1855 in Rome and went on to establish that same Third Order in Montreal. In their turn, the Sisters of Providence have spread devotion to Our Lady of Sorrows all over Canada, the United States, Chile, Argentina, and Africa.

Not only did Bishop Bourget encourage his people to celebrate with fervour all the feasts of Mary already contained in the liturgical calendar, he added some feasts himself. These include the Sacred Heart of Mary; Our Lady, Help of Christians; the Most Pure and Immaculate Heart of Mary; the Betrothal and the Maternity of Mary; Our Lady of Good Help; Our Lady of the Seven Sorrows; Our Lady of All Grace; and Our Lady of Good Counsel. Not only that, but he established many associations and confraternities in honour of Our Lady. As well, he invited from France several religious congregations devoted to Mary and founded several himself in Montreal.

Bishop Bourget resigned as Bishop of Montreal on May 16, 1876, and was succeeded by Bishop Edouard-Charles Fabre. Eight years later, when the diocese was strapped by severe financial difficulties, he went around the diocese begging and reciting his Rosary in order to help the new bishop. An old man now, he celebrated his last Mass December 8, 1884, in honour of the Immaculate Conception of Mary.

Right up until his death on June 8, 1885, however, he attended Mass and went to Communion. The last words on his lips were, "O Blessed Virgin, I know that you know what is best for me."

Bishop Bourget's prodigious efforts to implant devotion to Mary are still bearing fruit today. It might be of interest to note in passing that, since the year 1960, June 8 has been celebrated at Madonna House as the Feast of Our Lady of Combermere.

The folds of Mary's mantle also billow eastwards to cover the Acadians, who are descended from the French settlers who did not go further up the St. Lawrence River, but settled along the Atlantic seaboard of Canada. When, in 1713, by the Treaty of Utrecht, Acadia was given to England, the Acadians, being Catholic and unwilling to submit to a Protestant king, were forcibly deported and scattered among the English colonies.

A century later many of them started drifting back and re-established themselves in Nova Scotia and New Brunswick. In 1881 the Acadians held a convention in Memramcook, New Brunswick, where they adopted Our Lady of the Assumption as their patron saint, although there were some who wanted to follow the lead of Quebec in choosing St. John the Baptist. Three years later, at their next gathering, they designed a national flag. Like the flag of France, it has blue, white, and red bars, with the addition, however, of a golden star in the blue area, representing Mary as *Stella Maris*, "Star of the Sea". At the same time they enthusiastically endorsed the hymn "Ave Maris Stella" as their national anthem giving it a special melody all their own.

The Acadians began to thrive again and became the majority in three dioceses of New Brunswick: Moncton, Bathurst, and Edmunston. It is in Moncton that the beautiful cathedral of Our Lady of the Assumption was built in the 1930's and 40's by Archbishop Louis-Joseph Melanson, who earlier had founded a religious community called the Daughters of Our Lady of the Assumption. Every facet of the cathedral testifies to the central place that Our Lady holds in the lives of the Acadians. The nave, in particular, has a marvellous series of ten stained glass panels depicting women from the Old Testament who were prefigurations of Mary.

Our Lady's sphere of influence was not, however, limited to New France and Acadia. It was a dynamic force reaching outwards to the rest of the country. During the 18th

Century, many heroic and enterprising discoverers opened the great Northwest of Canada, a huge area of some 2,000,000 square miles. One of the most famous of these is undoubtedly Pierre de la Vérendrye, who was born in 1685 and died in 1749. He and his celebrated *coureurs de bois* canoed and portaged their way from Montreal to the Rockies.

The *coureurs de bois* have a mixed reputation, but they were for the most part genuine heroes, strong men in a great, uncharted wilderness. Coming from good, Catholic families, with a devotion to the Mother of God, many of them married Indian women and produced a stalwart race in Canada, the Metis.

These same *coureurs de bois* accompanied Samuel Hearne on his journey to the Arctic Ocean in 1771 and Alexander Mackenzie in 1789, when he reached the Arctic Ocean through the delta which bears his name.

The first two permanent missionaries to the West, Fathers Joseph-Norbert Provencher and Joseph-Nicholas Dumoulin, left Montreal on May 19, 1818 to establish a mission at what was to become St. Boniface. Three years later, Father Provencher was consecrated bishop. A few priests joined him, and gradually missions were established in the Northwest. One of the most celebrated missions in the West is the one dedicated to St. Anne, which was founded in 1844 by Father Jean-Baptiste Thibault at what became known as Lake St. Anne. The native people were quick to embrace a devotion to the grandmother of Jesus.

It seems that St. Anne and the diocesan clergy were preparing the way for the epic evangelization of the Northwest by the Oblates of Mary Immaculate, a new congregation founded in Marseilles by St. Eugène de Mazenod. Apostolic giants, the Oblates of Mary Immaculate were rightly named after Our Lady. For 100 years they and the native people were great friends. Missions flourished everywhere, and Canada was evangelized from sea to sea, even as its Latin motto proudly declares: *A Mari Usque Ad Mare.*

One cannot sing the praises of the Oblates and their devotion to Our Lady without mentioning the selfless dedication of many Sisters from many different congregations, particularly the Sisters of Charity, who established schools and hospitals at nearly every mission post during the 19th Century.

In the 1940s, however, as more and more white men penetrated into the North, many sins were committed against the native people. Thanks be to God that now the native nations are beginning to reclaim their languages and their cultures, so as to take their rightful place in the Canadian mosaic. Canada will not achieve peace until her native people are reconciled with both the French and the English, as well as the other nationalities which constitute a multi-cultural Canada. Let us turn to Mary, in her Immaculate Conception, and beg of her to repair all harm that has been done to the native people by the white race. The Mother of all our nationalities, she alone can obtain from the Holy Spirit a change of heart for us all, allowing us at long last to forgive and love one another.

On Pilgrims, Shrines and Our Lady of the Rosary

Today, millions of people travel; tourism is an international phenomenon. Feverishly we run here and there in pursuit of happiness, excitement, and novelty. Whether we know it or not, we are really seeking the Absolute. Deep down our hearts are yearning for the only One who can give us real happiness. The pilgrim is simply a person who consciously knows and acknowledges this. Of set purpose, he seeks the Absolute in his travels.

A shrine is a church or other sacred place visited by the faithful who come as pilgrims to show their special devotion and to be touched by the Absolute. A pilgrimage is a journey made by the faithful to such a place. The urge to go on pilgrimage to a holy place, a place set apart where we can experience the Divine in an immediate way, is part of our human nature. From time immemorial all cultures and religions have revered significant places as shrines.

When Jesus took on human flesh, he confirmed this aspect of our nature, sanctifying many places in first century Palestine by his divine presence. That's why we call it the Holy Land. Shrines have a special "vocation" in salvation history. Just as God calls each of his creatures to a specific mission in this life, so does he designate shrines in his Church throughout the world for particular purposes, tailoring these purposes to the needs of his people. The lives of many saints and great servants of the Lord both known and unknown were renewed and re-directed by pilgrimages to shrines, where their hearts were touched by an outpouring of grace.

The concept of pilgrimage has once again grown popular in our postconciliar times. We have a heightened awareness that we are a pilgrim people en route to our eternal destiny. The Second Vatican Council reminded us that we are a pilgrim Church.

Actually, only in the postconciliar period has any thought been given to defining the concept of shrine or to developing official criteria about shrines. We find no reference to shrines in the 1917 Code of Canon Law, in the writings of Vatican II, or even more recently in Pope Paul VI's instruction on proper devotion to Mary, entitled *Marialis Cultus*.

Nonetheless, it was Pope Paul VI who did try to remedy this situation. He called emphatically for serious reflection on the role of shrines in the life of the Church. At the first meeting of rectors of Marian shrines in Italy, Paul VI urged them to "lift their voices and let their existence be known in the Church."

In his annual addresses to the rectors of Marian shrines, during the course of meetings which they themselves had initiated, Paul VI was concerned with the meaning of shrines and their place in the liturgical and pastoral life of the Church. He described shrines as "spiritual clinics" (1965), "testimonies of miraculous deeds and of a continual wave of devotion" (1966), "luminous stars in the Church's sky... centres of devotion, of prayer, of recollection, of spiritual refreshment" (1970). He recommended in fact that shrines have a full program of sacramental and pastoral activity, and that they be centres of genuine religious fervour. He made it clear that devotion is an extension of liturgy and a preparation for it, that all Christian worship leads to Christ.

Before these addresses by Paul VI, academic theology had given scant consideration to shrines. Shrines had no formal or canonical Church recognition. It was Paul VI who instigated the legislation on shrines contained in the 1983

Code of Canon Law, which now guides the Church. Canons 1230-1234 define shrines as sacred places of pilgrimage, animated centres of intense Christian life which foster liturgical and sacramental practice and cultivate sound devotion.

While Eucharistic celebration and devotion are clearly in evidence at noted shrines like Lourdes and Fatima, all popular shrines offer the sacrament of reconciliation and the Eucharistic Liturgy regularly for pilgrims. Many shrines are also able to celebrate processions with the Blessed Sacrament and Benediction.

When the bishops' conference of the former Yugoslavia met in Zagreb, Nov. 18-27, 1990, to review events at Medjugorje, they decided to assist the local bishop "in organizing the pastoral activity in Medjugorje so that a proper liturgical and sacramental life may be promoted." In this way, they reasoned, pilgrims would be well served, even as the episcopal examination of the phenomenon continued. This is the situation that prevails today.

The Central committee for the 1987-1988 Marian Year issued an instructional letter on the mission of Marian shrines. Among its directives, the instruction encouraged shrines to present in the Eucharistic celebrations "a genuine image of the nature of the Church and of the Eucharist" and to "reveal the fullness of the paschal mystery, communion with the universal Church, and the presence of Mary in word and symbol."

Further, it encouraged shrines:

- to cultivate the *via pulchritudinis* or "way of beauty", that is to say, a sense of the beauty of God and Creation as manifested in and through Mary;

- to provide an atmosphere for discerning and responding to vocation as a gift of God; for a shrine is a sign of this mysterious relationship between God's call and the person's response;

- to be associated with or to sponsor a work of charity, such as a home for the sick, a school for the disadvantaged, a retirement center;
- to foster ecumenical prayer, encounters, and dialogues.

Marian shrines are a particular expression of devotion to Mary. In the last quarter-century especially, they have made enormous strides in promoting the liturgical and pastoral life of the Church.

Many shrines and religious congregations have had proper Masses particular to their respective histories and orientations. The rectors of shrines petitioned the Holy See to gather the best of these Masses and to compose new Masses in honour of our Blessed Mother. This concern for a richer liturgical life resulted in the composition of the *Collection of Masses of the Blessed Virgin Mary*, which was published in 1986 in two volumes, consisting of a Sacramentary and a Lectionary.

This collection of 46 votive Masses is wonderfully crafted in the spirit of the conciliar liturgical renewal and contains an abundant tradition of Marian veneration, with texts drawn from numerous historic and contemporary sources. This superb liturgical resource may be used almost any day by those on pilgrimage.

This initiative by the directors of shrines has enriched the liturgy of the whole Church, for the use of these special Marian Masses is extended to all parishes and communities seeking various votive Masses for a Saturday commemoration of Our Lady or for a special occasion.

A pilgrimage or visit to a sacred place honouring a significant event is intended to be an action both profoundly human and religious. Millions each year frequent the great historical locations where their country's grand events were forged. The concept of pilgrimage is prominent in all of the world's major religions: Christian, Jewish, Muslim, Hindu, and Buddhist.

The spirit of the early and medieval Church inspired pilgrimages to Jerusalem and Bethlehem, to the tombs of the apostles and martyrs, to the holy places of Rome, and to churches and shrines holding relics of saints. Internationally famous for pilgrimage in the Middle Ages were Saint James of Compostela in northwest Spain and Canterbury in England.

The Marian apparitions of the 19th and 20th centuries at Paris, Lourdes, La Salette, Knock, Beauraing, Fatima and other places created noted centres of prayer and renewal, intensifying devotion to Our Lady and revitalizing the spirit of pilgrimage in the Church.

In the Catholic world of today about 80 percent of all shrines are dedicated to Mary! Annually the vast majority of pilgrims turn their steps towards Marian shrines. For example, about ten million go to Guadalupe in Mexico, six million to Lourdes in France, five million to Czestochowa in Poland, and four million to Aparecida in Brazil.

A pilgrimage to a shrine is not a sightseeing visit. Rather, it is an exceptional effort that people make to break away from the routine of their lives and journey closer to God. Ordinarily pilgrims have endured privations in joining with others en route to a common goal. In a special communion that transcends time, they unite with pilgrims of the past in prayer and gratitude for a hallowed place. A pilgrimage is really just a smaller mirror image of the great journey of human life towards God, for the life of the Christian is indeed a pilgrimage. Ours is a pilgrim Church, journeying towards the heavenly kingdom.

All the actions of a pilgrimage are meant to be symbolic, instructive, and transforming: the preparation, joining together with other pilgrims, the welcome at the shrine, the visit to the sanctuary, the celebration of the Eucharist, the return home. The purpose of the pilgrimage is to guide the pilgrim "to the essential: Jesus Christ, the Savior, the end of every journey, and the source of all holiness."

Vatican II spoke of Mary's "pilgrimage of faith." She precedes and encourages us in our own pilgrimage of faith. Marian shrines are one expression of Mary's presence among us, the Church. In *Mother of the Redeemer*, his Marian year encyclical, John Paul II refers to a "geography" of faith and devotion to Mary which includes those special places of pilgrimage where the People of God find the one who first believed as well as a strengthening of their own faith. In a sense, too, God made Mary his first and greatest shrine. She is the place where we meet the Lord in a special, intimate way, for she nurtured him in her womb for nine months.

In today's world, with millions of refugees and displaced persons, shrines are becoming gathering places for people uprooted from their homes and churches. At the first World Congress on Shrines and Pilgrimages in 1992, sponsored by the Pontifical Council for Migrants and Itinerant People, John Paul II expressed the desire that "persons whom life has treated harshly, the poor, the people who are distant from the church" may find a welcome at shrines.

Hospitality extended to migrants and to all pilgrims at Marian shrines is an expression of the Virgin Mary's openness to God's word. Her example reminds all people that we come together in the great pilgrimage of life on this earth as we journey to everlasting life in our permanent home with God.

Canada's first settlers came across the ocean from a land that was full of the Catholic traditions and culture of the Middle Ages. In the Old World, veneration for Our Lady was woven into their day-to-day lives. The angelus bell of their parish or a nearby monastery would mark a break for prayer, as they toiled in their fields and workplaces. Tales of Mary's love for her children and legends of her miraculous interventions would have been handed down from generation to generation as they gathered around cottage hearthfires. Over the centuries there came to be many local shrines that were dedicated to her, which people would visit to ask for various blessings. They might seek a blessing for their harvest or an ailing child, or they might come to pray for rain in a drought, to seek deliverance in times of pestilence and famine, or to give their heart-felt thanks for the favours they had received.

Old Catholic France was steeped in an atmosphere of pilgrimages and shrines. This was true even of Old Catholic England, which was so Marian that it was called "Our Lady's Dower". During these ages of faith the roads of France and England were full of pilgrims on foot, both the high-born and the lowly, all dressed alike in their plain, distinctive garb, complete with a flat hat, satchel, and staff. For many of them their destination was one of the great and popular shrines of Our Lady, where they would seek her powerful intercession in a spirit of penance and prayer.

Among the oldest of these shrines was the shrine of "Our Lady Under the Ground" in a crypt of the cathedral at Chartres. This site dates back to pre-Christian times, when Druids held their rites there. Legend has it that at that spot the early Christians found a statue of a woman and child above an ancient altar. With the altar and statue they discovered an amazing, prophetic inscription, which paid tribute to "the future Mother of God who is to be born". Throughout the Middle Ages, all the kings of France paid homage to the Mother of God at this shrine.

At this time too, the shrine of Our Lady of Roc Amadour was considered so important that it was classed with the Holy Land, Rome, and St. James of Compostela as one of the four chief places of pilgrimage in the Christian world.

Not too far from the present-day site of Lourdes is the mountain shrine of Our Lady of Le Puy, which was probably the focal point of Marian devotion in France during the Middle Ages. Here too the Druids had had an altar. Later, the Romans erected a temple to their god, Jupiter, on the same spot. Afterwards, in the fifth century, Pope Gelasius I commissioned a Roman nobleman to design and build a shrine to Our Lady there. By the eleventh century, it had become famous throughout Christendom and a magnet for pilgrims, including seven popes. This sanctuary has been venerated by at least eighteen French kings and numberless princes and nobles. Charlemagne stopped there to venerate Our Lady on the way to and from his coronation by Pope Leo III in Rome. One of the region's great bishops, Adhemar of Montheil, is thought to have composed the *Salve Regina* or "Hail Holy Queen", which was known as the "Anthem of Puy". St. Dominic, St. Louis de France, St. Vincent Ferrer, St. Anthony of Padua, and St. Hugh are among the saints who have visited Our Lady of Puy. Huge, crowded pageants were held in Mary's honour there. Even as late as 1853, a throng of more than 300,000 people came to this shrine to venerate her.

Not only do we meet Our Lady at her shrines, but also in that grace-filled cycle of prayers we know as the Rosary. The pioneers brought this very important Marian devotion with them to the New World. During the sixteenth century the Rosary took shape and blossomed in its present, commonly-known form. For instance, it was only in the year 1568 that the second half of the Hail Mary, beginning with "Holy Mary", was endorsed officially. Before that the Hail Mary ended at the word, "Jesus".

Over the centuries, there had been many ways of saying the Rosary. One way was to say 150 of these shortened Hail Marys in imitation of the 150 psalms that priests and religious recited as part of the Divine Office. This kind of rosary was called "Our Lady's Psalter" or "the poor man's breviary." Another approach was to say a number of Hail Marys in order to offer them up as a garland of spiritual roses to the Queen of Heaven. This is how we get our word Rosary, which originally meant a wreath of roses. Since these "Hail Mary" roses were like a head-covering or crown for Our Lady, another word for the Rosary was chaplet, meaning "little hat". This is a word that is still used in both English and French. Oftentimes the Rosary would consist of 50 Hail Marys, although there were 63 in the so-called Bridgettine Rosary and 72 in what was termed the Franciscan Crown.

The Catholic faithful of Europe took to the Rosary in all its varieties with great fervour, latching onto its beautiful simplicity, which fit so well with the daily round of their lives, especially in the New World with its many dangers and hardships. With time they discovered that the beads of the Rosary made it easier for them to meditate on certain mysteries of the Faith, such as the five Wounds of Jesus, for instance, or the Sorrows and Joys of Our Lady.

The diocese of Paris, from which so many of Canada's early colonists came, was the first in Christendom to require all the faithful to learn the Hail Mary, as well as the Our Father and the Creed.

By the time New France was being colonized there was finally a consensus that the Rosary should consist of 150 Hail Marys in three groups of five mysteries each, namely, the Joyful, the Sorrowful, and the Glorious. The importance of the Rosary was further solidified by the great Christian victory at the Battle of Lepanto on October 7, 1571, which saved Europe from foreign invasion and was attributed to the intercession of Our Lady through the Rosary. Afterwards, Pope Saint Pius V commemorated this day by designating October 7 as the Feast of the Holy Rosary.

The Rosary is the ideal Marian prayer. By means of the Rosary Our Lady is held up as the gateway to her Son in all the aspects of his redemptive mission. Through this simple prayer, like a mother, she leads us deeper into the mysteries of his love for us. It was certainly providential how the Rosary was firmly established and popularized at this particular moment in history, for Mary was just the helper the colonists and missionaries needed as they confronted the perils of the raw wilderness, bringing Christ to a New World.

Our Lady of the Cape
Canada's National Shrine

Canada's national shrine to Our Lady of the Rosary is situated at Cap-de-la-Madeleine, Quebec, near Trois-Rivières (Three Rivers), on the St. Lawrence River. Known as Our Lady of the Cape, it is frequented by hundreds of thousands of pilgrims each year.

On October 7, 1535 Jacques Cartier planted a large, beautiful cross there. Beginning in 1616, Franciscan priests served the Indians and French traders "at the three rivers". In 1651, on November 21, the Feast of the Presentation, Jesuits took up residence there. The area's first wooden chapel was built in 1659 on land granted to Pierre Boucher, which he named "Fief Ste. Marie". The early inhabitants were so fervent in their faith that a brief entry in the Jesuit *Relations* for 1663 likens their community to a monastery, calling it an academy of virtue. In 1694 a Confraternity of the Holy Rosary was first established at the Cape, planting the seeds for what was to be the special theme of the later shrine. In 1714, on the authority of Bishop Saint-Vallier, the first wooden chapel was replaced by a stone chapel, still standing to this day as part of the shrine complex.

In 1729, with the death of Father Paul Vachon, who had been the pastor for 44 years, the parish at Cap-de-la-Madeleine lapsed into a period of darkness and decline, without a resident priest for the next 115 years. In 1844 a resident pastor was finally re-appointed to the Cape, only to find many parishioners fallen away from the practice of their faith and antagonistic to the Church. Like Christ himself, the parish had to go through the bitter experience of Calvary and the Tomb before its resurrection.

The resurrection came with the appointment of a holy new pastor, Father Luc Desilets, in 1864, ten years after one of the parishioners, Zépherin Dorval, had donated the statue of Our Lady which in later years would come to be called miraculous. In 1867, three years after his arrival in the parish, Father Desilets, weighed down by the apathy of his parishioners, experienced a moment of supreme discouragement. One day, he happened to enter his church, only to find a dirty pig snorting and scrambling onto the steps of the altar that housed the statue of Our Lady. In its jaws the pig carried a Rosary, which it had trampled and soiled. Retrieving the Rosary, Father Desilets drove the pig out of the church. Humiliated and desperate, he turned to Our Lady and made a vow to promote the Rosary in his parish and in the diocese. As a result, the parish was revived and began to be known far and wide as a centre of devotion to Our Lady.

By 1879 a much larger church was required to meet the needs of the parish. Stones had been prepared for it on the south side of the St. Lawrence River, the Cape being on the north bank, one mile across. All winter long the parishioners waited and prayed for the river to freeze, in order to transport the stone across the gap of water on top of an ice bridge with teams of horses. There are some years, however, when conditions do not allow the river to freeze. The winter of 1879 was shaping up to be one of those occasions. January and February had come and gone, but still the river had not frozen over. By the month of March, spring was in the air, and it seemed that only a miracle would give them the corridor of ice that they needed. The parishioners became doubtful and despondent, even as Father Desilets and his assistant, Father Duguay, held fast to their belief that Our Lady would come through for them and answer their prayers. Indeed, Father Desilets had vowed that, if the river froze and the stones were able to be brought over, he would dedicate the original church, which the parish had outgrown, to Our Lady of the Rosary. Suddenly, at the eleventh hour, on the eve of the Feast of St. Joseph, against all expectation, the weather changed, enabling the men to haul the stones across the river on a miraculous bridge of ice, which was attributed, not to a freak pattern of the weather, but to the rosaries that had been constantly said for days and days.

The first pilgrimage to Our Lady of the Cape was made on May 7, 1883. Blessed Frédéric Janssoone, who was a dynamic preacher, had a great influence in spreading devotion to Our Lady of the Cape in the early days of the shrine.

On June 22, 1888, at the formal dedication of the old stone chapel to Our Lady of the Most Holy Rosary, Father Frédéric said prophetically that, "In years to come, this will be the shrine of Mary. Pilgrims will come here from all the families of the parish, from all the parishes of the diocese and from all the dioceses of Canada. Yes, this little house of God will be too small to contain the crowds that will come to invoke the power and the bounty of the sweet Virgin of the most Holy Rosary."

On the evening of this same day, Father Desilets and Father Frédéric went over to the church to pray with a cripple named Pierre Lacroix, who explains what happened:

"I went into the shrine about 7 o'clock in the evening, accompanied by Father Desilets and Father Frédéric. I was walking, supported by them. We went to place ourselves at the communion rail. The priests were kneeling and I was seated behind them, for I could not take any other position because of my infirmities. After praying for a while, I looked up at the statue of the Blessed Virgin in front of me. Immediately I saw that her eyes were distinctly open in a life-like manner as if she were looking over us, towards Trois-Rivières. I examined this without saying anything. Then Father Desilets who was at my right, left his place and went over beside Father

Frédéric. I heard him say. 'Do you see it?' 'Yes,' answered Father Frédéric. 'The statue has opened its eyes, hasn't it?' 'Well yes, but has it really?' Then I told them that I had been seeing the same thing for several moments."

To Father Desilets, who had been longing for some confirmation, this "Prodigy of the Eyes" was an answer to prayer. Our Lady had hallowed this particular place and statue with her presence. Father Desilets told his curate, Father Duguay, "God wants this work. If you do not do it, you will die and God will raise another in your place. Father Frédéric will help you. It is not without the special design of providence that he is here." Father Desilets himself died two months later, his work of preparation accomplished.

After that the shrine's reputation grew rapidly, and more and more pilgrims each year visited Our Lady of the Cape from all over Canada, the United States, and other parts of the world.

The holy places of Palestine are particularly honored at Cap-de-la-Madeleine because it was in those holy places that the mysteries of the Rosary had their setting. The first organized pilgrimage from the United States came on August 3, 1893 from Cohoes, New York. The first documented cure took place on September 1, 1895, when a 15 year old girl was cured of her blindness.

In 1900 Father Frédéric had a wooden Way of the Cross erected at the shrine. By 1902 the Oblate Fathers of Mary Immaculate became the permanent guardians of the shrine and are still giving extraordinary service there today. They improved the grounds and built a basilica and a retreat house.

In 1904, by order of Pope Pius X, the statue of Our Lady of the Cape was crowned in the presence of most of the Canadian Bishops. The Plenary Council of Quebec, which was held in 1909, declared the Cape the national shrine to Our Lady for Canada. In 1994, the 300th anniversary of the erection of the Confraternity of the Rosary at Cap-de-la-Madeleine was celebrated.

Here, as at Fatima, our Lady brings her people back to God through the Rosary. Hundreds and hundreds of letters flow into the shrine, naming specific favours people have received through the intercession of Our Lady of the Cape. A young girl crippled for 10 years attends the blessing of the sick on the great feast of the Assumption and then goes home to find herself walking as if she had never known injury. A teaching sister who lost her voice for several years drinks water from Our Lady's spring and her voice is restored on the instant to its old vigour. A blacksmith comes to the shrine on crutches with a mangled leg. Later he returns to the shrine all healed, walking briskly, on vacation from his blacksmithing job, in order to leave his crutches at the shrine of her who restored his strength. A hopeless ailment disappears, a son returns, a father is cured of a sad addiction, a mother avoids a serious operation, a child is called back from the edge of the grave, the sorrowing are comforted and healed, and the despairing are filled with hope.

During Ottawa's celebrated Marian Congress in 1947, Our Lady of the Cape was specially honoured, and afterwards for four years the pilgrim statue of Our Lady of the Cape toured Canada from sea to sea. At the time I was a curate in a country parish in Morinville, Alberta, when the pilgrim statue came with two Oblate priests. Every service was thronged with the faithful.

A Special Pilgrimage to Ottawa

In our lives there are events which stand out as special occasions of joy. One such occasion for all the Catholics of Canada was the Marian Congress held in Ottawa, June 18 to 22, 1947.

I was on my way there by train when a gentleman approached me, saying "The Minister of Education from Alberta would like to speak with you." I went over to his compartment, where I was greeted warmly by the Honorable Earl Ansley, a man of great integrity, who explained, "I need your help. I'm the official representative of the Alberta Government to the Marian Congress in Ottawa and I haven't the slightest idea of what it's all about." So I took him under my wing.

I remember the splendid opening ceremonies at Notre Dame Basilica, as I pointed out the major figures in the entrance procession to Mr. Ansley. I can still see Archbishop Vachon, who had been inspired to organize this congress, smiling and happy, walking down the aisle towards the altar. Cardinal McGuigan of Toronto was the papal legate to the Congress and the main dignitary at all the major events. As well as hundreds of bishops, priests, and nuns, and thousands of the faithful, several cardinals came. Of these Cardinal Mindszenty, primate of Hungary, struck me as the most heavily burdened, for he knew that, when he returned home, he would be imprisoned by the Communists.

Another fascinating figure was Mar Ivanios of the South India Syro-Malabar Rite, who had joined the Catholic

Church with most of his diocese in the early 1930's. Also, members of the Young Christian Workers Association from 47 countries were present, as their convention was slated to take place in Montreal immediately after the Congress.

There were receptions of all kinds for the dignitaries, while the rest of us took great joy in the wonderful plays and other activities that were scheduled. A religious exhibition was held in Lansdowne Park, where a special Mass was celebrated. There was also a parade with floats depicting the life and apparitions of Our Lady. All kinds of music and singing in honour of Our Lady were featured. Among the singers were the boy choristers of St. Michael's Cathedral, Toronto. Also on the agenda was a solemn prayer of Consecration to the Immaculate Heart of Mary, followed by the prayer of Consecration of Canada by two prominent politicians. Cardinal Gerlier gave the French sermon and Cardinal Mooney, Archbishop of Detroit, the English sermon. The Congress ended with an evening procession of the Blessed Sacrament and solemn Benediction.

Surely the time is ripe for another Marian Congress in Canada!

Bench Marks: Our Lady in Canada 1900–2000

The twentieth century dawned brightly for Marian devotion in Canada, fuelled by the spiritual power of Our Lady's apparitions at Lourdes, La Salette and other places, not to mention her strong presence at shrines like the one at Cap-de-la-Madeleine in Quebec.

In Paris, on November 27, 1832, Our Lady gave the celebrated Miraculous Medal to St. Catherine Labouré. On one side of it was Our Lady of the Immaculate Conception; on the reverse side were the Sacred Hearts of Jesus and Mary. The lay people thronged to join a confraternity dedicated to the Sacred Heart of Mary. By 1900 there were 20 million members, many of them in Canada.

As the century grew older, more and more parishes were dedicated to Our Lady. For instance, from 1900 to 1920, 125 parishes were given her name under one title or another. Also, following the directives of Pope Leo XIII, Blessed Frédéric Janssoone launched the practice of celebrating October as the month of the Rosary at Cap-de-la-Madeleine. This practice spread and was adopted throughout Canada until Vatican II.

Early in the 20th Century, the Montfort Fathers established a Marian Center in Montreal, where an extensive Marian library was assembled. From there speakers went out to preach Marian devotion, especially in the Province of Quebec. A shrine was built in Montreal to honour Mary Queen of all Hearts. Some 4,000 pilgrims come to pray there every Sunday.

Reinforcing the widespread popularity of Our Lady of Lourdes, the apparitions at Fatima in 1917 further set the tone for the new Marian age that was beginning. Our Lady of Perpetual Help was also made popular, notably through novenas and parish missions conducted by the Redemptorists. Here are some of the milestones of this new Marian age in Canada:

1899 Confraternity of Mary Queen of Hearts was established on March 25 by Archbishop Joseph Thomas Duhamel, first archbishop of Ottawa, who had taken as his episcopal motto, "Draw us, Immaculate Virgin". Promoting consecration to Jesus through Mary, this confraternity spread to nearly all the parishes of the diocese and was adopted throughout Canada. A review dedicated to Mary Queen of Hearts has been published since 1904.

1903 All of Canada joined St. Pius X in celebrating the 50th anniversary of the Declaration of the Doctrine of the Immaculate Conception in 1854.

1903 Quebec City. The *Annals* of Our Lady of the Sacred Heart were born.

1904 The foundation of four religious orders of women took place:
- in the Archdiocese of Ottawa, the Servants of Jesus-Mary, under Fr. Alexis-Louis Mangin, who was strongly influenced by St. Louis de Montfort,
- Missionaries of the Immaculate Conception under Délia Tétreault (Mother Marie of the Holy Spirit),
- in the Saguenay, the Antonians of Mary, Queen of the Clergy,
- in St. Boniface, Manitoba, the Oblate Missionaries of the Sacred Heart and Mary Immaculate.

Bench Marks: Our Lady in Canada, 1900–2000

1910   Ottawa. The Grotto of Our Lady of Lourdes was built, drawing thousands of pilgrims annually.

1910   The celebrated Montreal Eucharistic Congress took place, in which Mary played a prominent role.

1929   From June 12-16, a great Marian Congress was held in Quebec City, its theme being "The Universal Mediation of Mary".

1931   On Oct. 11, Pope Pius XI instituted the feast of Mary, the Mother of God, now celebrated on January 1.

1932   The first praesidium of the Legion of Mary was founded in Canada by Father Walter Neway on Vancouver Island among the Cowichan, a tribe of native people. From there the Legion spread across the country.

1933   On April 7, Archbishop McGuigan of Regina and all the bishops of Saskatchewan consecrated their dioceses to the Blessed Virgin Mary.

1935   On May 8, six young women, with episcopal approval, founded the Association of Our Lady of Victory in Quebec City to propagate devotion to the holy Rosary.

1942   The Bishops of Quebec consecrated their dioceses, their parishes, their clergy, religious and faithful to Our Lady.

1942   Celebration of the 300th Anniversary of the foundation of Montreal, the "City of Mary", featuring a prayer to Our Lady of Montreal.

1946   A Canadian Marian center was established in Nicolet by Roger Brien. From here, for 15 years, he published what may have been the most magnificent magazine ever devoted to Our Lady, simply entitled *The Mary*

Journal*. The best theologians, writers, and artists contributed to this extraordinary masterpiece, which has never been excelled.

1946 -48 Father Patrick Peyton conducted extremely successful family Rosary crusades for the London diocese (1946), the whole of Saskatchewan (1947), and all the Northwest (1948).

1947 I personally witnessed an extraordinary event in the spiritual history of Canada at the Marian Congress of Ottawa. All the different activities culminated in the consecration to the Immaculate Heart of Mary, written by Pope Pius XII, read by the Prime Minister of Canada, Louis St. Laurent, in the presence of nine cardinals, thousands of priests, bishops, archbishops and a crowd estimated at 500,000 people. One of the fruits of this Marian Congress was the establishment of the Canadian Society of Marian Studies.

1948 In April in Montreal two women, Marie-Thérèse Chevalier and Gabrielle Lefebvre, dedicated their lives to the spread of devotion to Our Lady, especially through the printed word.

1950 A very successful Rosary crusade was held in the provinces of Quebec and New Brunswick, as well as eastern Ontario. A total of 65 percent of Catholics promised to recite the Rosary daily. Even some radio stations broadcast the Rosary daily.

1950 On November 1, Pope Pius XII proclaimed the dogma of Mary's Assumption into heaven.

1951 Madonna House, in Combermere, Ontario, became a Marian Apostolate where all who visit are encouraged

---

* original French title = *La Revue Marie*

to consecrate themselves to Jesus through Mary, according to the teachings of St. Louis de Montfort. Devotion to Our Lady of Combermere grew and took full flight on June 8, 1960, when Bishop William Joseph Smith of Pembroke blessed the statue of Our Lady of Combermere which stands on the grounds of Madonna House overlooking the beautiful Madawaska River.

1954   This was celebrated as a Marian year at the request of Pope Pius XII, who proclaimed her "Queen of the Universe". The Canadian bishops responded with enthusiasm, and everywhere across Canada conferences and sermons were given on true devotion to Mary.

1962   On October 11, the Second Vatican Council opened in Rome, having been placed under the protection of Our Lady.

1964   At the end of the Council, Pope Paul VI declared Mary Mother of the Church. The Council Fathers had included a brilliantly developed section on the Blessed Virgin Mary in the document on the Church called *Lumen Gentium*.

During the years following Vatican II, there was a great decline of Marian devotion in Canada. Few seminaries offered courses in Mariology. The Rosary was no longer being said in parishes and families. Few Marian theological studies appeared in the years that followed. One exception to the decline was the founding of the newspaper *Jesus, Mary, and Our Times**, in 1971, by Marie-Thérèse Chevalier. Also, during the conciliar and post-conciliar years, Father Henri-Marie Guindon did much to try to revive devotion to Mary by his writings and preaching.

---

* original French title = *Jésus, Marie, et Notre Temps*

Ukrainian Catholics, on the other hand, not only remained faithful to Marian devotion, but grew more fervent in their attachment to Mary after Vatican II, one great advantage of theirs being the beautiful icons of Our Lady in their churches.

1973   A large annual bus pilgrimage began, touring 17 Montreal churches and other regions of Quebec, with pilgrims praying the Rosary along the way.

1984   Quebec City. Sister Ghislaine Boucher, R.J.M., founded the Society of Mary Immaculate, which publishes, among other things, a remarkable journal entitled *Marian Sources of the Canadian Church**.

1987   Pope John Paul II proclaimed a Marian year as a preparation for the celebration of our redemption in the year 2000. The Canadian bishops responded with enthusiasm. Since then, devotion to Our Lady has been gathering new momentum, preparing people with joy and fervour for the second millennium. As St. Louis-Marie de Montfort said, "It is through Mary that the world's salvation began and it is through Mary that it must be consummated."

---

* original French title = *Aux Sources Mariales de l'Église Canadienne*

The Orthodox Church and Mary

The venerable Eastern Church has led the way in fostering devotion to the Mother of God. The first prayer to Our Lady, which dates from the third century, came to us from the East: "We turn to you for protection, Holy Mother of God. Listen to our prayers and help us in our needs. Save us from every danger, glorious and Blessed Virgin."

It was in the East that the great Council of Ephesus took place in A.D. 431, declaring Our Lady to be the Theotokos or Mother of God. Some of her most significant feasts were being celebrated in the East long before they were in the West. These include the Presentation of the Lord, the Dormition, the Annunciation, and the Nativity of Mary.

One of the most sublime Eastern prayers in honour of Our Lady is the Acathist Hymn, which was composed by Romanos the Melodist around 532. The word "Acathist" comes from the Greek and means that, when the hymn is sung, the people of the congregation do not sit, but stand to acknowledge God's majesty.

"All the figures under which she has been represented in the Scriptures are repeated here, in the second part, not in the form of a dry enumeration, but as applied to her by the living people of the Gospel, who thus participate in the universal concert of praise and personally glorify the Virgin Mary... it always brings us back to theological truth: to the fact that Mary is great because she is the Mother of God, the bridge between heaven and earth, for her intercession is all powerful with God, her Son. Her holiness and beauty are such that even the angels in their glory fall in admiration before her."*

From the earliest centuries in the East Mary has been venerated through her holy Icons. These include the theme of *Hodigitria*, in which Our Lady is portrayed as Guide of the Church, pointing with her hand to the Child Jesus. There is also the *Eleusa* cycle of icons, among which are those of Our Lady of Tenderness, the best known being the icon of the Mother of God of Vladimir. We have the *Enthroned* Mother of God, holding the Child on her lap. As well, there is the *Mother of God of the Sign*, who takes her name from the following Scripture passage: "Therefore the Lord himself shall give you a sign. Behold a Virgin shall conceive and bear a son and shall call his name Immanuel" (Isaiah 7:14). In addition to these, there are several other types of icons. There is even an icon of the *Theotokos, Joy of Canada*, venerated at the Monastery of All Saints in Dewdney, B.C., with a special acathist hymn dedicated to her.

Wherever an Orthodox community exists today, you can be sure that the Mother of God is highly honoured. According to a certain tradition, the first Orthodox Christians in Canada were native people of the Yukon. The story goes that a Russian priest converted them to Orthodox Christianity after the foundation of the Orthodox Mission in Alaska in 1794. When he left them, he cautioned, "Some priests will come in the future. You will recognize them as true priests if they venerate the Eucharist and the Mother of God." It may be that some Oblate Missionary in the 19th century met descendants of these Christians.

Other Orthodox Christians came to Canada later. After the Canadian Pacific Railway was finished in 1885, the railroad conducted an extensive advertising campaign all through

---

*Byzantine Daily Worship, by Most Reverend Joseph Raya and Baron José de Vinck (Allendale, N.J.: Alleluia Press, 1969) p. 959.

Europe to lure immigrants to the vast reaches of Canada. These Europeans came west, with many Orthodox people among them. The first Orthodox Liturgy was celebrated in Canada in 1897 at Wostok, Alberta.

Of the 750,000 Orthodox Christians in Canada today, 300,000 belong to the Greek Orthodox Church. There are some 150,000 members of the Ukrainian Orthodox Church, while the rest of the total number of Orthodox Christians in Canada belong to the Russian Orthodox, Serbian Orthodox, Romanian Orthodox, Bulgarian Orthodox, and Antiochian Orthodox Churches. All told, some 75 Orthodox churches in Canada are dedicated to the Mother of God. St. Michael's Parish at Gardenton, Manitoba, the first Ukrainian Church in Canada, is the site of an annual pilgrimage.

The Western Church has been enriched by borrowing from the liturgy and devotions of the Eastern Church. Let us pray that eventually, through the intercession of the Mother of God, Eastern and Western Christians may become one in our country and everywhere. "Rejoice, O Theotokos, Joy of Canada."

Mary's Love for Canada Revealed in Her Saints

St. Joseph, Husband of Mary, Patron Saint of Canada

As the spouse of the Blessed Virgin Mary, St. Joseph is most worthy of his role as patron saint of Canada, which is home to St. Joseph's Oratory in Montreal. The world's greatest shrine in his honour, it is a testimony to the simple faith and holiness of Blessed Brother André, who died on January 6, 1937 at the age of 91. A humble Holy Cross brother, he spent much of his life as a lowly doorkeeper, calling tirelessly on the intercession of St. Joseph to aid the poor, the sick and the afflicted. Because of Blessed Brother André's fidelity and vision, what began as a small, wooden chapel on the mountainside is now a huge basilica perched high on the northern slope of Mount Royal, visited yearly by more than 2,000,000 pilgrims who come to pay homage to St. Joseph, the Church's noblest image of earthly fatherhood.

At the moment of the Annunciation the angel Gabriel brings the good tidings to Mary, telling her that she is to conceive the Son of the Most High. To which Mary answers, "How can this come about, since I am a Virgin?" (Lk 1:31-34).

Mary's answer indicates that she and Joseph had both already consecrated their virginity to God. As many reputable Catholic scripture scholars have concluded, she would not have been betrothed without that common pledge. Undoubtedly, Joseph loved her deeply and missed her terribly during the three months she spent with Elizabeth. Imagine his shock and consternation when she returned and he saw that she was pregnant! It would have made no sense to him, for already he knew her too well to believe she could have been unfaithful. Scripture tells us how an angel of the Lord, appearing to him in a dream, shed light on his predicament, saying:

"Joseph, Son of David. Do not be afraid to take Mary home as your wife, because she has conceived what is in her by the Holy Spirit. She will give birth to a son and you must name him Jesus, because he is the one who is to save his people from their sins" (Mt 1:20-22).

Immediately Joseph believed the angel "and took his wife to his home and, though he had not had intercourse with her, she gave birth to a son and he named him Jesus" (Mt 1:25). The act of self-surrender God called him to make at that moment was like the faith expected of Abraham when he was ordered by God to sacrifice his son Isaac. All the patriarchs and great people of the Bible lived by faith, trusting totally in the Word of God.

Joseph guided and protected the little family of Nazareth, providing for all the needs of his wife and his adopted Son. Joseph was indeed Jesus' male role-model. His marriage to Mary was a real marriage, not merely a make-believe arrangement. While they were not united in body, they were more totally united in heart and mind and soul than any couple has ever been.

Fathomless mysteries lie waiting to be discovered, as we contemplate the relationships between Jesus, Mary and Joseph. In the case of Jesus, who was Holy Wisdom personified, the Son of God and the Son of Mary, we can conclude that he gave more glory to God by his obedient submission to his foster-father and mother than by his miracles. The example of Jesus teaches us that it is the humble, little things we do that count.

By virtue of her Immaculate Conception and divine motherhood Mary was favoured with the greatest possible graces. In her holiness, wisdom, and knowledge, she was far above Joseph. The great fathers of the Church grope for words in their attempt to describe her. Being so close to God, Mary was able to love Joseph as no other husband has ever been loved before or since.

Joseph was not immaculately conceived, but came into this world like each one of us, with the stain of original sin on his soul. Like us, he had an inclination and great capacity for sin. Nevertheless, in close communion as he was with his divine foster-son and his immaculate wife, God granted Joseph immense graces. Because of his holiness and capacity for love, he is the patron of the universal Church. No father has ever been more tenderly paternal towards a son. No husband has ever been so loving and understanding of his wife.

Traditionally St. Joseph is associated with *silence*. Small wonder! He must have enjoyed such an intense spiritual exchange with the other members of the Holy Family that it took all his listening skills to absorb even a small portion of it. We can be sure that his knowledge and wisdom grew by leaps and bounds in the company of Jesus and Mary. Without a doubt St. Joseph was a great theologian, for he lived day by day with the Man-God, coming to know and love him as no other man has before or since. As for his wife, he loved her and shared with her the wonders of God, not just in words, but by an intimate spiritual communion not ever experienced by any other couple.

St. Joseph listened and obeyed, doing all that God desired of him. He is to be revered as the best of fathers, the most loving of husbands, furnishing all husbands and fathers down through the ages with a supreme example to imitate. Also, by his long years of toil in the carpenter's shop St. Joseph has ennobled the vocation of the working man.

Tradition has it that he died peacefully in the arms of Jesus and Mary. For this reason, he has also become the patron saint of a happy death, helping us to pass over from this world to the next.

His intercessory powers are immense. In heaven Joseph gives all his petitions to his wife in a wordless communion and she, in turn, begs her Son to grant his "father" everything he asks for. Whenever you pray to Joseph, you are praying to Jesus through Mary. He is the most Marian of saints!

Saints of the Founding Phase

Joseph Chiwatenhwa (1602?–1640)
First Native Lay Apostle

Joseph Chiwatenhwa was a Huron Indian who had been instructed personally by St. Jean de Brébeuf and baptized by him in Huronia on August 16, 1637, when he was about 35. He soon became a model to all the believers of this new church, preaching Jesus Christ boldly, even in the Indian councils.

The first native lay apostle, he was a man of prayer and had an instinctive horror of sin. One of his elegantly simple prayers was, "You who have made all, you are the master of the animals. If you make some fall into my trap, may you be blessed. If not, I want only what you want."

His wife, Marie Aonnetta, and her family also became Catholics. They were referred to as "the family of believers". At the time of his wife's baptism, Joseph declared to the people present, "My brothers, I am pleased to have you know that my wife is entirely resolved to believe in God and to serve him, and that, from now on, she abandons forever all the superstitions of the country in order to be baptized." Joseph and his wife were married at the same ceremony and received Holy Communion.

Some of his sayings illustrate the depth of his faith:

"Alas, how insignificant is the support of men. Those who loved me the most in the world and from whom I derived most, my father and my mother, have died. God alone in his goodness has served me as father and mother. When I was in no way thinking of him, he thought unceasingly of me. This great God has called from the end of the world and from beyond the seas men (missionaries) who have come for me and for me almost alone; how great, my God, is your love. Shall I lean on another than you?"

"I no longer fear death at all and I would thank God if I saw myself at the end of my life, in the firm hope that I have of going to heaven. In like manner, I am no longer apprehensive of the death of any of my relatives, provided they die in the grace of God."

On August 2, 1640, Joseph was killed by marauding Iroquois. His death was a great blow to the missionaries. St. Gabriel Lalemant remarked that, "Since the saints have more power when they are in heaven than here below on earth, we are bound to believe that we have gained more than we lost by his death."

His family continued to be faithful Christians. His niece, Theresa Oionhaton, became known as the Flower of Huronia, following in her uncle's footsteps.

The Jesuit Martyrs (17th Century)

On the 4th of July, 1634, two Jesuit missionaries visited the area later known as Trois-Rivières, which became a jumping off place for them and others. From here, under Our Lady's protection, they travelled further afield into more dangerous regions to bring the message of Christ. Their zeal was to be tried through many hardships, even to the point of a martyr's death. These two bearded blackrobes were Jean de Brébeuf and Antoine Daniel, the future saints.

These priests were soon followed by the superior of the Jesuits in Canada, Father Paul Le Jeune, who had assigned himself to this new mission of Trois-Rivières. With him he brought the man who was to be the great missionary of the St. Maurice region, Father Jacques Buteux, S.J. Arriving on the Feast of Our Lady's Nativity, September 8, they consecrated the mission to the Immaculate Conception, a tribute to Mary which has been a hallmark of Trois-Rivières through the centuries.

The Jesuits moved quickly towards Georgian Bay and established themselves in Huronia, where they called their mission St. Marie, to honour Our Lady, who was their patroness in New France.

Of the first eight French missionaries to undergo martyrdom in Canada, six were Jesuits and two were laymen whom we today would call permanent volunteers. Three were killed at Ossernenon, the present-day site of Auriesville, N.Y., and five in Huronia, 200 kilometers north of Toronto.

Having come from France in 1640, the layman, René Goupil, was on his way to the Huron mission with Father Isaac Jogues and about 40 Hurons, when they were captured by the Iroquois on Lake St. Peter. Father Jogues was tortured and mutilated, while René Goupil suffered a deadly blow at Ossernenon, on September 29, 1642.

Managing to escape, Father Jogues, who was named "Bird of Prey" by the Indians for his zeal and courage, returned to France and later came back to the new world. With Jean de la Lande and a few natives, Father Jogues left Trois-Rivières for Huronia on September 24, 1646. Stopping at Ossernenon, they were received there with great mistrust by the Iroquois, who thought that the religion of the black-robes was responsible for the illness which had caused many deaths in the village. Father Jogues met his end by a blow to the neck on October 18, 1646, Jean de la Lande being killed the following day.

Father Antoine Daniel, a native of Dieppe, disembarked in Quebec in 1633. For seven years he directed a school for young Hurons. Afterwards he followed Father Jean de Brébeuf into Huronia. On July 4, 1648, the Iroquois attacked the Jesuit mission of St. Joseph, located south of St. Marie, just as Father Daniel finished Mass. They pierced his body with arrows and many rifle shots and then threw it into the burning chapel.

Father Jean de Brébeuf, who hailed from Normandy, arrived in Quebec in 1625 and spent the winter in the forest with the Montagnais Indians to learn their way of life. A giant of a man in every way, beloved by his flock, he was stationed at the Huron mission from 1626 to 1629, then was later reassigned to it from 1634 until his death. Father Brébeuf, a man of deep prayer, had made a vow to accept martyrdom, desiring to be crucified in imitation of Christ. Like Our Lady, he was completely submissive to the will of God.

He and Father Gabriel Lalemant, who had come to New France in 1646, were captured in Huronia by the Iroquois and taken to St. Ignatius Church, about two miles from Midland, where they were each tied to a post and tortured. The Iroquois were intent on testing their courage and breaking them, as they would an enemy brave, until they flinched and cried out under torture. Both Father de Brébeuf and Father Lalemant proved courageous beyond anything that had ever been seen by the Iroquois. Father Brébeuf endured his torture for three hours, dying March 16, 1649, after an unparalleled display of bravery and eloquence. It is believed by some historians that at times during his ordeal he went into complete ecstasy and felt nothing, coming out of this state twice to preach Christ to his torturers, who admired him so much that, after his death, they cut out his heart and ate it in the belief that they could acquire some of his courage this way. Years later, when missionaries went to the Iroquois, one of them said, "I was evangelized by Father de Brébeuf, while he was being tortured." Father Lalemant had been in Huronia only six months when he met his end with Father Brébeuf. He died on March 17, 1649, his agony lasting 15 hours.

Father Charles Garnier, born in Paris, reached Quebec in 1636 and was immediately stationed in Huronia. His mission post was attacked by the Iroquois on December 7, 1649.

While Father Garnier was bringing the sacraments to the dying, he was shot twice, then axed to death.

Father Noël Chabanel, the son of a wealthy wine merchant in the Haute-Loire region of France, had arrived in Quebec in 1643 and worked in the missions of Huronia. Father Chabanel detested everything about Canada and life among the Hurons. Though he had been a brilliant scholar back in France, he found himself utterly incapable of learning the Huron language. Nevertheless, he made a vow to remain forever at the mission. After that, he was able to say with great peace, "I do not know how God will dispose of me, but I feel completely changed. I am naturally apprehensive, but now that I'm facing the greatest danger and know that death is probably near, I have no more fear. This time, may I give myself to God forever." On December 8, 1649, while he was escorting a group of homeless Hurons to one of the mission posts, the Iroquois attacked the travelers, who scattered in terror. Father Chabanel was killed in the melee by an apostate Huron, who threw his body into the river.

All these missionaries came freely to Canada, ready for martyrdom, with an all-embracing love for Our Lady and the native people. They spent time earnestly assimilating the culture of the Hurons, living among them and learning their language.

Of these heroic men, Blessed Marie of the Incarnation wrote to her son in the fall of 1649:

"They possessed the very spirit of the Word Incarnate. It is this spirit which drives the apostles of the Gospel to rush by earth and sea and makes of them living martyrs before iron and fire consume them... It makes one feel and experience the spirit of the eight Beatitudes..."

Blessed Catherine of St. Augustine (1632-1668) Co-foundress of the Canadian Church

Catherine de Longpré was born in Normandy, France on May 3, 1632 and baptized the same day. Given over to the care of her grandparents, she tried to avoid sin from early childhood. One day she asked a Jesuit priest the question: "Who is good at doing the will of God?" The priest pointed to a poor man, who was covered with ulcers and vermin, and replied, "My child, this poor man is very good at doing the will of God, for he patiently accepts his illness." What he meant was that we do a surer job of following the will of God in suffering than when we have everything our way.

For four years, starting at the age of four, Catherine used to speak to a picture of Our Lady, asking her advice and direction. "In my imagination," she wrote later, "I felt that this picture spoke to me. Because of that, I called it my Blessed Virgin and I did nothing without asking her permission. I told her everything. I asked her for her advice more simply, more frankly, more tenderly, than even to my mother, and she treated me with the caresses and love of a mother."

At a very early age Catherine understood the value of suffering. When she was five, for example, she endured violent headaches for three months without complaint. Aged ten, she composed and made her own act of consecration to Our Lady, signing it with her own blood on September 8, 1642. In 1643 she met St. John Eudes, who imparted to her a lifelong devotion to the Sacred Heart of Mary, which she was to help popularize in New France.

At 12 Catherine became a postulant with the Sisters Hospitallers of the Mercy of Jesus, turning always to Our Lady with total trust. Going to communion, she would say, "O Mother, full of love, when you received the Body of Jesus Christ, your divine Son, what was your heart saying?" When she served the poor, she would exclaim, "With what humility, O Holy Virgin, with what gentleness, what joy did you fulfill this same office?" While doing the ordinary domestic jobs of sweeping, cooking, and washing dishes, she asked herself, "What were our Lady's interior dispositions while performing the same chores?" In suffering, she would say, "In similar encounters the heart of Our Lady was gentle, humble, and patient. May mine be like unto yours, O Holy Virgin."

With a deep desire to go to Canada, she completed her novitiate on April 25, 1648. Four months later, on August 19, 1648, aged 16, she arrived in Quebec, where she was to work the rest of her life, for 20 years, as nurse, bursar, director-general, and mistress of novices.

From her station in Quebec she offered herself as a victim soul to lessen the burdens of the Canadian missionaries. While she suffered intensely from interior temptations, she was always favoured with many mystical graces, which included consoling visions of Our Lady. Because of her consecrated victimhood, she is considered a co-foundress of the Church in Canada.

In 1665 she made a vow: to always do what she knew to be most perfect, to seek only what would serve the greatest glory of God. Even though she was often beset by illness, she was always an image of joy and peace in her service of others. Catherine was a strong woman, given to decisive action and devoted to her faith, spreading joy and consolation to her patients with great tenderness. She was open, frank, and generous, and her writings show that she had excellent common sense and a lucid spirit of discernment.

On her deathbed Blessed Catherine renewed the offering of her will to God, praying, "Oh my God, I adore your divine perfections. I adore your divine justice and I abandon myself to it with all my heart." She died May 8, 1668 and was beatified by Pope John Paul II more than three centuries later, on April 23, 1989.

Blessed Marie of the Incarnation (1599–1672)

Blessed Marie has been called the Teresa of New France. Like St. Teresa of Avila, she was both a practical woman and a great mystic.

Marie Guyart, who was born in Tours, France, on October 28, 1599, married a silk manufacturer with the surname of Martin at the age of 17. After only two years she was left a widow, with a son to raise.

In 1631, persuaded that she had a religious vocation, she entered the Ursuline Monastery at Tours, entrusting her son, Claude, now 12, to the care of her sister. As hard as the parting was, Claude corresponded regularly with his mother once she left for Canada in 1639. Eventually he became a Benedictine and five years after her death wrote her first biography.

Under strict spiritual direction she quickly grew in grace and soon achieved the most advanced stages of prayer. Not too long after she had entered the convent, Claude ran away and went missing for three days before he was found. Later on she wrote, "O God, I would never have believed that the grief of a mother for the loss of her child could be such torment... All this happened in the octave of Epiphany, during which was being sung the Gospel that told of Mary's loss of the Boy Jesus in the Temple."

Towards the end of 1633, while still in Tours, she had a dream. In it she and an unknown lady were walking towards a harbour. Then they took a boat and, as she explains, "we arrived finally at a vast country. Having disembarked, we climbed a hill by a route about the width of a wide door.

"...We came to a little church. There was an embrasure on the roof fashioned in the shape of a seat on which the Holy Virgin sat. As soon as I glimpsed Mary, trembling with pleasure and dropping my friend's hand, I ran towards the Blessed

Mother. I extended my arms in such a way that they were able to touch the two ends of the little church on which she was seated. I saw her look at her Blessed Infant. Without speaking, she communicated something of importance to my heart. It seemed that she was saying something about the land and about me and that she had some design in regard to me and I, I was longing for her, so I was reaching out my arms. Then with a lovely grace, she turned to me, smiling affectionately. She kissed me without saying a word. Then she turned back toward her Son and again she communicated with him wordlessly. I knew within me that she had some plan for me and that she was speaking of it to him. Then she kissed him again. Again she silently addressed her son. Firmly she kissed me a third time, filling my soul with gladness by her caresses, a gladness and a sweetness that are indescribable."

A year passed before she understood that the land of her dream was New France. She wrote, "Again I felt a great interior attraction for that country and with it, a command that I should go there." She heard the words, "It is Canada that I have shown you. You must go there to build a house for Jesus and Mary." Later she reflected on this instruction, pondering the close-knit nature of the Holy Family: "I had it in my heart that Jesus, Mary and Joseph would never be too far from one another. So much so that one time when I was at table in the refectory, overwhelmed with affection for them, I said, 'O, my love, this house must be for Jesus, Mary and Joseph.'"

On the way to Canada their little ship, called the *St. Joseph*, was miraculously preserved from collision with an iceberg by prayer to Mary.

In 1645 she made a vow of perfection, resolving to live it out under the protection of the holy Mother of God. It was followed by a long period of great darkness. In 1647, on the Feast of the Assumption, she explains, "I had a strong inspiration to petition my dear Mother to grant me deliverance (from the darkness) if it would glorify her beloved son. I was near the Blessed Sacrament at the time. In an instant, I felt my prayer answered, and the pall lifted from me like a garment. Then peace overflowed my inmost being, and my aversions were changed into heartfelt affection."

When her convent burned to the ground, the nuns heroically saved all the children in their charge by turning to Mary. All Quebec helped them in the work of reconstruction, again with the help of Our Lady.

"All the aversion that I had felt for redesigning our convent disappeared," Marie relates. "I was strong and full of courage in the pursuit of all I had to do. I looked upon the whole affair as belonging to the Virgin, our Mother and superior. I no sooner undertook something than I felt her assistance in an extraordinary way. Continually, she was present. I experienced her without seeing her. She was nearby, accompanying me everywhere as I came and went, from the time of clearing away the ruins, until the building was finished."

In another testimonial to Our Lady, she wrote, "One day when we were burdened with many debts and had no means of paying them off, I was in dread of upsetting the persons concerned. While I was thinking about the situation, I received a letter from France, which before opening I carried to the feet of the Blessed Virgin. There I recommended our finances to her and told her that I was awaiting her help. In the letter I found that the Queen, in her goodness, had sent us an alms of 2,000 livres."

Marie never separated devotion to the Sacred Heart, the Word Incarnate, from devotion to the Heart of his Mother. It is evident from her writings that her approach to Our Lady revolved around two great realities: Mary as Mother of God and Mary as Mother of Mankind. From 1635 on, she wore a small iron chain around her neck as a sign of the vow of service that bound her to Our Lady. In 1668 she penned these words about her patroness in heaven: "This divine Mother of ours is a great help to us. In all our needs she is there to assist us, keeping us safe, like the pupil of her eye. It is she who upholds our family in a hidden, but effective, way. She takes all our concerns on herself... what is there that I should fear when I am sheltered under the wings of such a kind and powerful protectress?"

Marie offered God her prayers, works, and sufferings for the good of the Church in New France and everywhere. She died peacefully on April 30, 1672, after a long and painful illness, which she gladly offered for the native people. She was beatified by Pope John Paul II on June 22, 1980.

Jeanne Mance (1606-1673) and Ville Marie

The visionary quest to found Montreal, the City of Mary, began with a layman in France, Monsieur Jerome le Royer, Sieur de la Dauversière, who was "instructed by God" to establish a colony on the Island of Montreal. He gathered around him several of the well-known people of his time, mostly lay people, along with three priests, the most celebrated being Father Jean-Jacques Olier, founder of the Sulpicians. In full, they called themselves the Society of Our Lady of Montreal. On February 27, 1642, the members of the Society met at Our Lady's altar in the church of Notre Dame in Paris in order to "consecrate the Island of Montreal to the Holy Family, Jesus, Mary, and Joseph, under the particular protection of Our Lady", as a contemporary account puts it. To lead the actual establishment of the colony, they chose a layman, Paul de Chomedy, Sieur de Maisonneuve, and a 34-year-old laywoman, Jeanne Mance.

Jeanne had desired to come to New France after reading the so-called *Relations*, accounts of the work the Jesuit missionaries were doing in the New World. Second in a family of twelve children, she was raised as a devout Catholic and was endowed with an orderly mind and gift for administration, which she coupled with a charming personality.

On May 17, 1642, when the pioneers set foot on the island, Jeanne set up the altar for the first Mass. Since she had medical knowledge, her main apostolate was nursing the sick, the first hospital being a room in her house.

Because of fires over the years, very few written records from the time of Jeanne Mance have survived, especially for the first years of her hospital, the Hôtel-Dieu. Unfortunately, the Hôtel-Dieu today possesses not a single signature or authentic portrait of its foundress in its archives.

Nevertheless, it is clear enough that she was an impressive personality, strong willed, practical, and austere, known too for her exquisite politeness. The annals of the Hôtel-Dieu of la Flèche explain that, "as she was of an attractive enough exterior and as she spoke of God as none could do better, a number of ladies of first quality took a pleasure in seeing her and conversing with her."

For the first few years, life in the little colony was quite busy, and everyone was happy, living inside a fort that Maisonneuve had built as a defense against the hostile Iroquois Indians. Later Jeanne was to look back on those days as idyllic. United in love and a spirit of mutual service, everyone helped in the common work of the settlement. No doors were ever locked, for example, and everybody attended Mass before going to work in the morning.

Jeanne faced many hardships, the main ones being political opposition, fear of the Iroquois, and poverty. The first of these probably caused her more distress than the latter two. The officials at Quebec City were reluctant to endorse a new colony so far away and unprotected, and she was under continual pressure from the ecclesiastical authorities of Quebec to yield control of the Hôtel-Dieu at Montreal to them.

Added to this was the gradual weakening of support from France. In 1649 she made her way to Quebec and found bad news awaiting her. For various reasons the Society of Our Lady of Montreal seemed to be in danger of breaking up, chiefly on account of the growing sentiment in France that the location of the fledgling settlement of Montreal was too dangerous. To make matters worse, Monsieur de la Dauversière, the manager of the hospital funds, was reported to be bankrupt.

The fate of the Montreal settlement depended completely on Jeanne at this stage. There was no one to advise her, for the people at Quebec had no sympathy with her in her troubles, and there was no time to go back to Montreal to consult with Maisonneuve.

Decisively, she sailed for France and succeeded in re-establishing support for the enterprise. Her courage and ability were never more evident. If she had not been willing to face the perils of another sea journey to encourage the failing enthusiasm of her friends, the whole venture would probably have gone to pieces.

The next year, she arrived back in Montreal, only to find that the Iroquois were pressing hard, threatening the very existence of the settlement. Jeanne herself nearly fell into their hands one day, when they captured some of the settlers working in the fields near the hospital, which was outside the fort. She was alone in the building, but some of the workers saved the day by holding off the onslaught. Another more determined attack on the hospital in July, 1650 caused Jeanne to be moved back into the fort.

Things got so bad that the very survival of the colony came into question. Men were being lost in the fighting and not being replaced. Maisonneuve desperately needed both money and men. Jeanne Mance gave him all she had, the 22,000 livres that had been set aside for the future hospital. Maisonneuve went to France for aid and two years later returned with a hundred men on leaky ships that were hardly more than disease carriers, bringing with him Marguerite Bourgeoys. She and Jeanne became fast friends.

In 1657, Jeanne broke her arm in a fall on the ice, an injury which disabled her for the next two years, eventually forcing her to return to France to seek help. In 1659, after an ocean journey of 71 days, she brought back with her three nuns, Hospitallers of St. Joseph, who formed the original nursing staff of Jeanne's hospital, the Hôtel-Dieu.

The Hôtel-Dieu was built of wood and stone in roughly equal proportions. The men's ward contained six beds and the women's two. There was a large fireplace at the end of the men's section that did for both wards. All the cooking was done in this fireplace, and the druggist had a corner there for his work. Here also the linen and dressings were washed and, more often than not, there were too many sick for the provisions available. The winter cold was a terrible hardship, which was compounded by a simple, spartan menu.

As this was the only hospital west of Quebec City, it had a wide territory to draw from. Frequently there were Indian patients, either friendly Hurons or even wounded Iroquois. The terror of the Indian attacks often taxed the new hospital staff to the limit.

Meanwhile, in the eyes of his superiors, Maisonneuve had failed, and control of the Montreal settlement of Ville Marie was given to the Order of St. Sulpice. Maisonneuve, a heroic figure, was sorely missed. One of his contemporaries, the keeper of the annals at the Hôtel-Dieu of Quebec, described him as "that faithful servant of Mary... the father and protector of the people that he governed."

In June 1672, Jeanne, whose health had been failing for some time, gathered enough strength to attend the laying of the foundation stone of the new Notre Dame parish church. In honour of her matchless contribution to the founding of Montreal, she was one of five people whose names were inscribed on leaden plaques set into the foundations, each of these plaques bearing the legend, "To our great, good God and to the Blessed Virgin Mary, under the title of her Purification". Dying on June 18, 1673 at the age of 67, Jeanne Mance was buried in the chapel of her hospital. She personified the original spirit of the Society of Our Lady of Montreal, of which Francis Parkman, the celebrated American historian, himself a Protestant, wrote, "None of the ordinary motives of colonization had part in their design. It owed its conception and birth to religious zeal alone."

Blessed Kateri Tekakwitha (1656–1680)

Kateri Tekakwitha was born in 1656 in Ossernenon, the present-day site of Auriesville, New York. Her mother, Kahenta (Flower of the Prairie), was a Catholic Algonquin from Trois-Rivières who had been a captive, while her father, Kenhoromkwa (Beloved), was a Mohawk chief.

In 1659-60 Kateri lost her father, mother, and baby brother to a terrible smallpox epidemic. Although Kateri survived, her eyes became weak, and her skin remained pock-marked for life. Despite her poor eyesight, she became very adept at sewing and embroidering.

Kateri was 10 years old when the French conquered the area, bringing with them Jesuit missionaries. Eighty of the villagers became Christians. Although her uncle, with whom she lived, was extremely bigoted against these missionaries, Kateri was much attracted to the new faith.

At the age of 20, having been well prepared by Jesuit Father Jacques de Lamberville, she was baptized. Because her relatives were quite angry and tried to induce her away from her faith, the priest wanted to remove her to a mission dedicated to St. Francis Xavier in New France near Montreal. The opportunity came when three lay catechists visited her village.

One of them, Louis Garonhiague, an Oneida chief, agreed to help her escape to St. Francis Xavier mission, which was a 200 mile trek.

At her new home Kateri's humility and love were soon evident. Spending long hours in church, she lived a life of sacrifice and mortification. Kateri's face grew radiant whenever she received the Eucharist. A lover of the cross, she carved it on a tree in the little oratory which she had made in the woods. She and Mary Teresa Tegaiaguenta, also a convert, became fast friends, praying and doing penance together.

On a number of occasions in her short life she was accused of unchastity, but each time she was vindicated. Having no desire to marry, she wanted to make a vow of virginity. In March of 1679 she approached her spiritual director with the idea. "This is a serious matter," he replied. "Take three days to think it over." Kateri was back to see him in 10 minutes. "I do not need any more time," she told him. "This has been the desire of my whole life."

On the Feast of the Annunciation, March 25, 1679, Kateri went to Mass, received Holy Communion, and then pronounced her vow, renouncing marriage forever and making Christ her only spouse. With her heart on fire with love, she asked Our Lady to be her Mother from that time on and to present her to her divine Son. By this single act she consecrated herself to Mary as well as Jesus. Henceforth, she only wore blue and was readily accepted into the Sodality of Our Lady.

Kateri died on Holy Thursday of 1680, after giving her friend, Teresa, this poignant message:

"I am leaving you. I'm going to die. Always remember what we have done together. If you change, I shall accuse you before God. Keep up your courage. Don't mind the sneers of those who have no faith. Listen to the Fathers. ... Never give up your penances. I will love you in heaven. I will pray for you. I will help you."

Her last words were, "Jesus, Mary, I love you." Within 15 minutes of her death, her face, which had been disfigured from smallpox from the age of four, was completely healed and became beautiful. Devotion to her slowly grew, until at length Pope John Paul II beatified her on June 22, 1980.

St. Marguerite Bourgeoys (1620-1700) Foundress, Congregation of Notre Dame

St. Marguerite Bourgeoys was born in 1620 in Normandy into a strongly Catholic family. At the age of 20, while walking in a public procession on the feast of Our Lady of the Rosary, she happened to look up at the stone figure of Our Lady on the portal of an abbey church dedicated to her, and something mysterious happened. She later described it as a "moment of grace (that) brought such a deep change in me that I felt I was no longer the same person." She knew then that her vocation was to promote God's glory and work for the poor.

In France she failed in her attempts to join the Carmelites and the Poor Clares and even tried unsuccessfully to found a religious order of women. After these reverses, her spiritual director advised her to imitate the missionary life of Our Lady and told her, "A person can still be a true religious without a veil."

She took this advice and, at the invitation of Paul de Maisonneuve, Marguerite left for Canada in 1653, when Ville Marie (Montreal) was scarcely more than a small fort. Calling herself "the family donkey", she spent herself tirelessly, easing the hard lives of everyone she encountered in the settlement. Marguerite wanted to promote a spiritual reign of the Blessed Mother in the hearts of children especially.

She founded schools and recruited helpers, not only in the colony but also in France, staying obedient to Bishop Laval, even though he did not understand her special kind of religious order, which was uncloistered and took only simple vows. It was only two years before her death that he finally gave his canonical approval to the Congregation that she had dedicated to "Notre Dame", Our Lady.

One of Marguerite's most lasting accomplishments was to build a chapel in honour of Our Lady under the title of Good Help, *Notre Dame de Bon Secours*, as she is known in French. It took 21 years, coupled with much prayer and patience on her part, for the chapel to be built and recognized by the bishop. The statue venerated at *Notre Dame de Bon Secours* is a replica of the famous six-inch statue of *Notre Dame de Montaigu*, which was discovered in the 16th century by a shepherd. In the end, the chapel became the place of pilgrimage and spiritual refreshment that St. Marguerite had envisioned. When the Hôtel-Dieu Sisters lost all their buildings in a fire in 1695, for example, they and members of the Notre Dame Congregation began to make pilgrimages to the chapel, entrusting their cares to Our Lady.

One of the very first women to join Marguerite in establishing the new Congregation was Marie Barbier, whose father had built and installed the celebrated cross at the top of Mt. Royal. Marie was a mystic, but also had practical common sense, as do all true mystics.

Marguerite used to say that in community everyone is expected to move without complaining from one task to another, as the need arises. Marie took the lesson to heart. She taught in the school like the others, but she was just as ready, whenever it was necessary, to herd the two cows over to graze on the common. Not afraid to turn her hand to anything she was asked to do, she took a big share in household responsibilities and became fairly adept at making butter and baking bread. Baking bread, she thought, presented the greater challenge, and she did not mind speaking openly about her many blunders, as when she made too much dough for the pans or forgot to add the yeast.

Slowly Marguerite's little congregation grew, with schools being established all along the St. Lawrence. When it came time to write constitutions, Marie Barbier wrote to the bishop: "I beg you, Excellency, to allow us to have no constitutions other than the life of the Blessed Virgin Mary."

To prospective candidates for her congregation, Marguerite would say: "love simplicity, humility and poverty. We firmly resolve to abandon the principles of the world, to live in the spirit of total renunciation of self and all things earthly; to seek only the glory of God; to be entirely devoted to the instruction of young girls, to the constant practice of all good works, without murmuring at the pain, trouble, and humiliation which are inseparable from these, but learning to love, to imitate the Blessed Virgin's life of simplicity and retirement in all things."

Marguerite herself lived heroically. She fasted, ate little, and drank only a bit of water every day, scarcely enough to quench her thirst, even as she exhausted herself in physical labour.

"How much we can gain by little acts when they are performed purely for God's love," she wrote. "He is contented, even pleased with our most trivial actions, provided they are done for his love... ."

At her death on January 12, 1700, a priest who knew her well wrote, "If the saints were canonized, as in the past, by the voice of the people and the clergy, tomorrow we should say the Mass of St. Marguerite of Canada." As it turned out, she was canonized on October 31, 1982, by Pope John Paul II.

Jeanne LeBer (1662-1714)
First Woman Contemplative in Canada

Among the many holy settlers of Ville Marie not yet beatified is Jeanne LeBer, who was born on January 4, 1662, an only daughter. Her father, Jacques LeBer, a wealthy businessman, had married Jeanne Le Moyne, who came from a distinguished colonial family. He was a man of faith and strong principles.

At 11, Jeanne was sent to the Ursuline Convent in Quebec City, where she stayed for three years. In her late teens, a talented young girl, she broke the news to her father and four brothers that she felt God was calling her to a life of solitude as a recluse. In 1680, Jeanne's spiritual director, a Sulpician priest, arranged for her to be established as a hermitess in a small apartment in her father's house.

Under spiritual direction, Jeanne followed a carefully balanced program of prayer, spiritual reading, rest, and work. As she was free to administer the sums allotted to her by her father, she donated money for the education of needy persons. She also helped the poor by sewing and knitting for them. In addition, she made and embroidered priestly vestments, tabernacle veils, and other altar accessories.

St. Marguerite Bourgeoys became friends with the little recluse. In 1694, when her convent burned to the ground, Marguerite was forced to replace the building. Jeanne LeBer asked if the sisters would be willing to add a tiny wing to the new chapel, having it directly connected with the sanctuary and permitting her to take residence there. Also, Jeanne offered to pay a considerable part of the cost of this chapel.

St. Marguerite's Congregation agreed to the proposal, and, in 1695, 15 years after her initial dedication, Jeanne moved to her new cloister. Priests and nuns, her relatives, as well as other families, all took part in the procession from the

LeBer home to the new dwelling and all of them understood that from this day forward they would have a faithful representative in prayer before the altar of the Lord. Throughout New France missionaries and settlers took courage from Jeanne's self-immolation for the glory of God and the good of the colony.

In her pursuit of holiness, Jeanne always followed the little way. Those who received permission to visit her may have expected a dramatic revelation of intense mystical experiences, but instead they found nothing exceptional. They saw a fervent contemplative, doing ordinary things within the context of her extraordinary vocation. This great simplicity enabled her to remain close to the people, who never ceased to think of her as one of themselves.

Like her father, Jeanne continued to make donations to charitable causes and to work for the poor. The vestments and altar ornaments which she embroidered with loving care were strikingly beautiful. People gazed on them in wonder, explaining the phenomenon of their exquisite craftsmanship by saying that the angels must have worked with Jeanne to produce them.

Jeanne was extremely close to her father. Although their formal visits with each other were few, their mutual understanding and affection were great. While Jeanne's mother had died several years before, she had another, more powerful Mother in heaven. Like all the people of Ville Marie, Jeanne was consecrated to Our Lady, who was present to Jeanne's every action, every moment of her life. Indeed, Jeanne's prayers to her were thought to have saved the colony from invasion by the English in 1711.

Jeanne died on October 3, 1714 at the age of 52. A congregation of nuns, the Recluse Sisters, follow in her footsteps even to this day in Montreal and Newfoundland.

No one has described the life and influence of Jeanne LeBer more movingly than an American writer, a Protestant lady named Willa Cather, in her celebrated book, *Shadows on the Rock*. Once, as I was going through a rough patch in my life, I re-read *Shadows On the Rock* several times. Each time I wept tears of joy, being especially moved by the references to Jeanne LeBer. She was intensely present to me in those days and brought me back into the sunlight.

If you visit the Marguerite Bourgeoys Centre in Montreal, you can see the sacred vessels that were donated by Jeanne for use in the chapel services. In the museum attached to the celebrated Notre Dame Church are the beautiful monstrance and other objects that were Jeanne's gifts to the parish, as well as the magnificent antependium and vestments that are the work of her hand and heart. If you go to the Musée St. Gabriel, you will be shown still other sacred vessels that were gifts from her. There you can also see the large cope she embroidered. If you are alone, the sisters may bring you a chair and invite you to sit for a time in front of this masterpiece, pointing out the marvelous preservation of the rich colouring, the exceptional quality of the silk, the beauty and strength of the silver thread, the evenness of the stitching, and so on. You may find that the longer you study the piece, the more inclined you will be to believe that the angels probably did have a hand in it, just as the people of her time supposed.

Saint Marguerite D'Youville (1701-1771)
First Canadian-Born Saint
Foundress, Sisters of Charity of Montreal

Marguerite was born in 1701 at Varennes, near Montreal. Because her father died when she was 7, she quickly learned to help her mother and take care of her brothers and sisters. At the age of 11 she was sent to the Ursuline Convent School in Quebec, where she received a wonderful education in both spiritual and cultural things.

A beautiful woman, she could have married anyone she wanted, but circumstances were such that she was espoused to François d'Youville. Soon she discovered that he was a harsh man, engaged in the illicit liquor trade with the native people.

At the age of 26, she received a tremendous grace, an insight into the fatherhood of God and his infinite love for every one of his children. Our Lady had led her quickly to Jesus, and Jesus in turn led her to his Father. The Father, in his Divine Providence, became a central facet of her faith and devotion. Later Marguerite would say, "For almost 40 years the Eternal Father has been the object of all my confidence," and "I leave all to Divine Providence. My confidence is in it."

By the time she was 30, she had suffered the loss of her father, her husband, and four of her six children. After her husband's death she gave herself tirelessly to the task of bringing up her two sons, both of whom eventually became priests. "Few mothers loved their children as tenderly as my mother," her son, Charles, wrote. Marguerite also cared tirelessly for all the poor, abused, and abandoned whom she came across.

In this work, three other women joined her on December 31, 1737. They soon formed a congregation, The Sisters of Charity of Montreal, better known as the Grey Nuns. As a community, their first act was to kneel before a statue of Our Lady of Providence and consecrate themselves to God, promising to serve the poor for the rest of their lives. They placed their work of service under Mary's protection.

The new little congregation was often misunderstood and persecuted by the people. They were falsely accused of selling liquor to the natives and of being drunkards themselves. In French, the word "grey" can also mean "tipsy," so that they became known as "the tipsy nuns." After a fire completely destroyed their home during the night of January 31, 1745, it was alleged that the nuns started the fire themselves, because they were intoxicated. Marguerite asked herself, "What can we learn from this? Perhaps we have been too well off. Now we will have to live more poorly. We ought not to be more comfortable than the poor."

Two days later they signed their founding document: "For the glory of God, for the relief of the poor, we are united in poverty and charity to live and die together, to consecrate without reserve our time, our days, indeed our entire life, to labour for, as well as receive, feed and support as many poor as we can take care of."

Meanwhile, the General Hospital in Montreal was falling into ruin and disrepair. Marguerite and her group were asked to take care of it. They did so for four years, renovating it during that time. Then, to their dismay, they were told to close it and send all their patients to Quebec City. "God be praised," Marguerite exclaimed. "We must carry our cross and he surely gives it in abundance."

Eventually, they were given permission to continue their hospital work and other apostolic labours in Montreal and finally, by 1755, they had both civil and ecclesiastical approval.

Marguerite, who was ever a practical woman, put two small farms of the hospital into cultivation and rented vacant land for pasture. She also planted a large apple orchard, which in due time became a good source of revenue. As well, she sold building stone, lime, and sand.

During the Seven Years' War between France and England, which began in 1756 and ended with a British victory in 1763, the Grey Nuns took care of all the wounded from both sides. On May 18, 1765, the hospital burned down during the great fire that came to threaten the whole city. Miraculously the hospital's painting of the Eternal Father was not touched by the fire, nor was the statue of Our Lady of Providence. Marguerite knelt down with her companions and recited the *Te Deum*. This time many came to her help, including the native people she had cared for during the smallpox epidemic of 1755. "In God, nothing is lost," Marguerite commented.

As she lay dying in 1771, Marguerite begged her sisters to follow the path God had chosen for them, to walk in the ways of obedience to the will of the Father and discover joy in selfless service. Above all she urged them to live in perfect union and charity. "To adore the designs of God and to submit to his will, that is what we have tried to do," she said. Marguerite died on December 23, aged 70.

The Grey Nuns quickly burgeoned as a religious order and are found today on nearly every continent. We in Canada are especially grateful to them not only for the work they have done in eastern Canada, but for assisting the Oblate Fathers so heroically all through the Great Northwest since 1850.

Marguerite d'Youville, the first Canadian-born person to be declared a saint, was canonized on December 9, 1990 by Pope John Paul II. This remarkable woman was known as the Mother of Universal Charity. The late Bishop William Smith, who was the ordinary of the diocese of Pembroke some years ago, once described her in this way:

"God designed Marguerite d'Youville to be, in the Church of the young colony, mother to the afflicted and abandoned. She was the strong woman in the Bible who opens her hands to the needy and stretches out her arms to the poor. Mother d'Youville's whole life was one of trials and crosses and anxieties. Her trials strengthened her spirit and she brought to her work a power of will and a zeal and devotion that heroic souls alone are capable of experiencing. This woman, fitted by nature and education to shine in society, devoted herself unflinchingly to the service of the poor and needy."

Saints of the Nineteenth Century

Blessed Marie-Rose Durocher (1811-1849) Foundress, The Sisters of the Holy Names of Jesus and Mary

Mother Marie-Rose Durocher was born October 6, 1811 and baptized as Eulalie-Mélanie. In her earlier years, she was given a good education by the Sisters of the Congregation of Notre Dame.

When her brother, Father Théophile Durocher, was named parish priest of Beloeil, not far from Montreal, he invited his father and sister, who was 19, to live with him in the rectory. She spent the next 12 years as his housekeeper, humbly looking after the needs of everyone who came to the rectory, which also served as a rest home for convalescent priests and seminarians. Eventually, Father Durocher asked another young woman, Mélodie Dufresne, to help his sister with her heavy responsibilities. The two women became fast friends, for they both harboured a deep desire for the religious life.

The two of them made and repaired church vestments and ornaments, helped with catechism, and prepared hot meals for the children who had to travel great distances. They also visited the poor and brought them food. Endowed with a solid practicality, Eulalie-Mélanie even formed a group of nurses' aides who visited the sick. As well, she took care of the religious education of young girls.

When the great Bishop Ignace Bourget needed priests and nuns for his Montreal Diocese, he approached St. Eugène de Mazenod, founder of the Oblates of Mary Immaculate. Bishop Mazenod sent him four Oblate priests and two brothers, including a certain Father Telmon. The latter founded the Congregation of the Daughters of Mary Immaculate and asked Eulalie-Mélanie to gather young women each week to pray and learn the rule of this new association. The young women made an annual covenant to avoid all worldly behavior and to be constant in the practice of their faith.

Eulalie-Mélanie recognized that there was a need for nuns to teach the children of the area. In October, 1843, under the guidance of Father Telmon, Eulalie-Mélanie Durocher and Mélodie Dufresne established the new teaching community of the Sisters of the Holy Names of Jesus and Mary in Longueuil, near Montreal.

The four postulants taught 13 boarders and 14 day students that first year. Prayer, teaching, and study marked their life. The day began at 4:30 in the morning with the recitation of the Little Office of the Blessed Virgin Mary, followed by Mass. Father Allard, another Oblate priest, gave them lectures on prayer and teaching, for none of them had been trained as teachers. A year later, Bishop Bourget gave the four postulants their habits and their new names in religion, choosing the name of Marie-Rose for Eulalie-Mélanie Durocher.

In 1834 Mother Marie-Rose had consecrated herself to Mary and had asked the Mother of Heaven to give her "the grace to become a good and fervent nun." Still aided by Our Lady now as foundress of a new community, she acquired the spiritual and cultural qualifications to assist her sisters in fulfilling the mission given to them by their constitution, which was: "To work for Christian instruction and the education of youth." With Mary's help, too, she led her nuns to make progress in meditation and prayer as they scaled the heights in their ascent to God. She herself attained that spiritual summit accessible to only a few souls, since it was her heart-whole desire to surrender herself totally to God with a love centred on him alone.

Because her love for Mary had always been so deeply founded, she named Our Lady as the first and foremost superior of her little religious community. When she found herself too burdened by her duties as acting superior to give the novices as much time as she would have liked, she confided these young Sisters to the direction of Mary Immaculate. When Sisters shared their anxieties with her and asked for advice, Mother Marie-Rose, after giving them her opinion, would often send them off to the chapel, adding, "Ask Our Lady to help you. Ask her to entreat her Son to let you know what you should do." At times she herself accompanied the troubled Sister, and together they would beg the help of the Mother of God.

In the early days, everything in the daily round of activities during the month of May was offered in her honour: classes, study, prayer, and evening devotions in particular. One of the few recorded prayers of Mother Marie-Rose is an Act of Consecration to Our Lady. Her correspondence with the sisters often ended with words like "united to you in the Sacred Hearts of Jesus and Mary," or "yours in Jesus and Mary".

Her twofold love is clearly seen in her preference for religious art which depicted the Son of God in the company of his Mother. A small statue representing Jesus in the arms of Mary was her favourite. Hers was a warm, personal devotion to Jesus and Mary, and she took a visible delight in adorning altars and shrines in their honour.

Her love of Jesus inspired her great reverence for priests. "If we had no priests, what would we do?" she asked. "Neither money nor whatever help we can give them will ever repay our debt to them for the spiritual benefits they bring to us." It was love of Jesus, too, that explained her great respect for ecclesiastical authority. "Enlightened faith made her see in her lawful superiors the representatives of Jesus Christ," commented Bishop Bourget.

Love was the virtue she was most keen to cultivate. With readiness and ease she would ask forgiveness of her Sisters for any fault of hers and was quick, in turn, to find excuses for their faults. Correction was administered by her with much kindness and discernment, for she was anxious never to extinguish the smoldering wick.

Regarding poverty, Father Allard warned them, "It is not difficult to practice poverty when you lack just about everything. Poverty safeguards you, but later, when your Congregation will begin to enjoy a certain prosperity, then poverty will become difficult. In order to observe it, you will need to have the love of and the spirit of poverty." Never a truer word spoken!

When Mother Marie-Rose Durocher died on October 6, 1849, she left the world a congregation consisting of about 40 nuns, 30 of them teaching nuns in the four houses of the Montreal diocese. After her death the community grew prodigiously. Today, her spiritual daughters teach in 300 institutions in Canada, the United States, the Cameroons, Nigeria, Lesotho, Brazil, Peru and Haiti. Pope John Paul II beatified her on May 23, 1982.

Marcelle Mallet (1805-1871)
Foundress, The Sisters of Charity of Quebec

Marcelle Mallet was born in Montreal, a descendant of Pierre Mallet, one of the colonists who had come to the City of Mary with Maisonneuve. Pierre Mallet, who died in 1711, had been a zealous member of the military brotherhood of the Holy Family, established in 1663, under the particular protection of Our Lady, to guard the new settlement.

From 1806 to 1815 Marcelle lived with her family and her maternal grandparents in the village of Assumption, about 20 miles northeast of Montreal. Like the village, the parish was dedicated to Our Lady of the Assumption. In 1810 Marcelle lost her father and her maternal grandmother. Because there was no Catholic school in town, she was home-schooled by her mother and her grandfather. Moving back to Montreal with her family in 1815, she took catechism instruction at the convent of the Sisters of the Congregation of Notre Dame.

After her confirmation in 1822, she gave herself over to work for the poor under the auspices of the Sisters of Charity (or Grey Nuns) in Montreal. Two years later, at the age of 19, she joined them and spent the next twenty-five years of her life as a religious at Montreal's General Hospital. This period of her life coincided with strong manifestations of Marian piety in the city. On June 2 of 1827, which Pope Leo XII had declared a year of jubilee, the Sisters dedicated themselves and their poor to Our Lady of Grace. Another great outpouring of regard for Our Lady came in 1847, at the height of the deadly typhoid epidemic, when Bishop Bourget moved to re-establish pilgrimages to the shrine of Our Lady of Good Help, asking for her intercession to put an end to the inroads of this terrible disease. The Sisters did their part to heed Bishop Bourget's initiative by making a novena to Our Lady of Good Help and visiting her shrine. During this time of crisis, Sister Marcelle worked tirelessly, nursing the sick and alleviating their distress.

Towards the middle of the nineteenth century the Grey Nuns were growing rapidly and were in great demand all over Canada. From 1840 to 1849 four groups left Montreal to establish separate communities of Sisters of Charity: one in St. Hyacinthe; another at Rivière-Rouge (St. Boniface, Manitoba); another in Bytown (Ottawa); and yet another in Quebec City.

In 1849 Sister Marcelle was chosen to found the new community in Quebec City. Firmly convinced that Mary was the way to Jesus, she was happy to find a great devotion to Our Lady already established there. At the centre of her spiritual life was the person of Jesus Christ, whom she contemplated in the mystery of his Sacred Heart. This was the characteristic note of her spirituality, which was reinforced by Our Lady, because nobody knew and loved "the good Master", as she called Jesus, better than did his Mother. It was Mary who helped Mother Marcelle to love Jesus. Mother Marcelle took great pleasure in leading her sisters on pilgrimage to the various churches and shrines found around Quebec City, especially the famous Chapel of Our Lady of Victories.

Mother Marcelle called Mary "my good Mother", considering her the superior of the congregation that she had established in Quebec City. She introduced the custom that required the new superior, after each election, to go to the statue of Our Lady and acclaim her in turn as the true superior of the community. She and her nuns celebrated all the feasts of Our Lady with great enthusiasm and love. Mother Marcelle herself fasted every Saturday in honour of Our Lady and inspired the nuns who were teachers to form their students well in a solid, unaffected devotion to Mary. Although Mother Marcelle was a woman of few words who did not put many of her thoughts in writing, her actions, all done in union with Mary, touched and fired her Sisters' hearts with a great love for the Mother of God.

Out of the small collection of Mother Marcelle's writings, the following prayer, written in 1867 and only found after her death, reveals quite strikingly her loving, childlike soul, which was so much like that of Saint Thérèse of Lisieux:

"I pray my Saviour and his holy Mother to take me under their divine protection and to obtain for their poor child the strength to practice the most perfect charity in all things. To obtain this great grace, I call particularly on my good Mother, the Blessed Virgin. O Mary, make me love and imitate the Sacred Heart of Jesus all my life. You can see it. My heart is attracted to you as a little child who cannot be appeased, except in the arms of his good Mother... Allow me, my august sovereign, to rush into your maternal heart and there, without words, as a child, I find my rest. For I know that you understand what I feel and what is the cause of my pain."

Mother Marcelle died on April 9, 1871, which was Easter Sunday, having put into practice that great principle of the spiritual life: to Jesus through Mary.

Mother Élisabeth Bruyère (1818-1876) Foundress, The Sisters of Charity of Ottawa

Born in Assumption, Quebec, on March 19, 1818, Élisabeth Bruyère was left without a father at the age of six. As the eldest of three children, therefore, she was called early in life to a spirit of sacrifice and self-giving. On the very day she received the Eucharist for the first time, in 1827, she consecrated herself to Mary before an ancient statue of her in the venerable church of Notre Dame in Montreal. At 12, she went to live with one of her mother's cousins, Father Charles-Thomas Caron, who was like a father to the young girl, encouraging her in her devotional life. At the same time, she was given the benefit of a first-rate education at the hands of her cousin, Émilie Caron, whom she loved with all the tenderness of a child for her mother. Later, Émilie was to become one of the founders of the Sisters of Providence.

On December 8, 1831, when Élisabeth was 13, she consecrated herself to both Jesus and Mary before a picture of Our Lady. At 16 she became a teacher in a rural school, then joined the Sisters of Charity of Montreal (or Grey Nuns), where she made her profession as a religious in 1841.

For about four years she was given charge of around 40 older orphaned girls, teaching and forming them. Then, at the extraordinarily young age of 26, she was chosen as the founding superior of a new house to be established in Ottawa, which, until 1855, was known as Bytown. The nuns had been requested by Bishop Patrick Phelan and the Oblate Fathers, for the specific purpose of running a school. On their departure from Montreal, Bishop Bourget told them it was their mission "to make the august Mother of God better known, loved, and served." Bishop Phelan, meanwhile, placed the founding nuns "under the special protection of the Most Holy Virgin, Mother of Mercy and Consolation of the poor and afflicted."

February 20, 1845 was a red letter day for the 3,125 Catholics of Bytown. The entire population was out and about in a festive mood and dress. The bells of the parish church, which was dedicated to Our Lady, rang out their greeting, while a picturesque procession formed for the triumphant entrance of the Grey Nuns into Bytown. The group, headed by Mother Élisabeth, was made up of four professed sisters, one novice, and a postulant. Three were French-speaking and three were English-speaking.

On the Monday morning of March 3, 1845, the dream of the pastor, Father Adrien Telmon, O.M.I., became a reality. The first bilingual school west of Quebec opened with 120 French-speaking and English-speaking pupils in a sturdily built cart shed.

Next, a hospital was built; then a boarding school for girls; then several more schools. None of this was accomplished without a strong spirit of trust in Divine Providence and the intercession of Our Lady. The nuns had to beg for everything. After a struggle, for example, the school board relented and gave one nun a salary of $100, but the other three teaching nuns received nothing.

Even at such a young age, Mother Élisabeth was a dauntless woman, full of faith, common sense, and Christian hope. In spirit and outlook she closely resembled the foundress of her community, St. Marguerite D'Youville. Like St. Marguerite, Mother Élisabeth had a great love for God the Father in his aspect of Divine Providence. Like her, she had a special devotion to the Hearts of Jesus and Mary and tried with all her strength to imitate the virtues of Our Lady, who was especially helpful to her under the following titles: the Mother of Jesus, Our Mother, Our Lady of Providence, Our Lady of Good Help, Our Lady of Mercy, Our Lady of Sorrows, and Refuge of Sinners.

This distinguished spiritual daughter of St. Marguerite was known for her universal love of the poor, the needy, and the sick, without distinction of race, colour or religion. With her sensitive understanding of the Mystical Body of Christ, she believed that in serving these she served Christ himself. Of the poor, she said to her nuns, "Remember that the moment we lose our love for the poor, we lose our distinctive spirit. You have promised to love Jesus in the person of the poor, the sick, and the children you teach."

In her quest for the Lord she modelled herself after Our Lady, who was totally receptive to the promptings of the Holy Spirit. Her relationship with the Blessed Mother was so close that, at the 1849 chapter meeting of the Grey Nuns in Montreal, like Mother Marcelle, she chose Mary as the real superior of her community. From this, the tradition arose among her Sisters to consecrate themselves each year to Our Lady. Also, as part of an effort to evangelize young people, the Oblate Fathers worked closely with Mother Élisabeth to establish the association known as the Congregation of the Children of Mary in the city's parishes, schools, and convent.

The promulgation of the Dogma of the Immaculate Conception on December 8, 1854 was celebrated with an outpouring of enthusiasm in her community, a beautiful statue of Mary Immaculate being placed in the chapel of the motherhouse. All of Bytown was caught up in the festive spirit and mounted a great celebration in honour of Our Lady. The nuns greeted each other joyfully with the words, "Hail to Mary Immaculate, the glory of our people. Let us rejoice mightily in this day that the Lord has made."

In 1856 the Constitutions of the Grey Nuns of Ottawa were written. In this document we read: "The first means the Sisters shall employ to enter intimately into the Heart of Jesus and to remain faithfully and constantly united to him will be a sincere and loving devotion towards his holy Mother." Keeping true to their Constitutions, Mother Élisabeth and her community honoured Mary in several ways. In the first place, the feasts of Our Lady were celebrated in a special, holiday spirit. Mother Élisabeth also encouraged processions and novenas in her honour. Pictures, paintings, and statues of Mary were found everywhere in her convents. To spread devotion to Our Lady, she distributed medals of the Immaculate Conception and the blue scapular.

Like a child, Mother Élisabeth loved her heavenly Mother, counting heavily on her intercession. On April 24, 1863, she wrote, in a spirit of humble expectation:

"During the coming month of May, we shall thank God for all the graces, temporal and spiritual, received this year through the intercession of Mary. We ask our good Mother to help us finish the hospital."

Besides seeking material favours, she quite often prayed to her for the spiritual growth of the community and for the needs of the Church everywhere. Her deepest instinct was to turn to her for everything. Every situation was ripe for her intercession. Mother Élisabeth would turn to her for all her needs: healings, protection during the typhus epidemic, the success of construction, safe travel, food, help for the working men, aid in building schools, hospitals, and houses, etc.

Mother Élisabeth Bruyère died on April 5, 1876 and was buried on April 7, the Feast of Our Lady of Pity.

Élisabeth Turgeon (1840–1881)
Foundress, Sisters of Our Lady of the Rosary

Élisabeth was born into a Marian family in Beaumont, Quebec on February 7, 1840. A physically frail girl, she was the fifth of 10 children in a family where the Rosary held a place of honour, as did processions and visits to a little area chapel dedicated to Our Lady.

In 1860 she left home for Quebec City, entering the women's section of the Laval Normal School, in order to be trained as a teacher. The principal of this normal school, as teacher training centres were called in those days, was a Marian priest named Father Jean Langevin, an outstanding catechist. There were three keystones in Father Langevin's spiritual approach, which he tried to pass on to his student teachers:

1. the importance of visits to the Blessed Sacrament,
2. a vivid appreciation of the maternal love of Our Lady,
3. the need as teacher to be devoted to the guardian angels of one's students.

The Ursuline nuns, with whom Élisabeth lived at this time, encouraged the imitation of Mary's virtues and stressed the importance of the Rosary, teaching her how to recite the Little Office of Our Lady, as well as various litanies and different forms of consecration to Our Lady.

After a three year stay at the normal school, Élisabeth's first assignment came in September, 1863, when she went to teach in St. Romuald. Very quickly she learned to entrust her children and her teaching to Our Lady, achieving astonishing success. It was soon clear she was an incomparable teacher, blending her natural talents with her deep devotional life. Even unruly children gradually became good students under her expert tutelage. Later she would share with her nuns the deeply Marian aspects of her teaching methods: "Let us invoke Our Lady under the title of Divine Shepherdess so as to place our students under her maternal protection. Let us try to inspire in them a tender devotion for this good mother."

After St. Romuald, she taught private classes in St. Roch, near Quebec City, and then opened a little free school near St. Anne de Beaupré. Twice during those years, severe illness brought her to the very brink of death. She survived and harboured a vague notion that God still had some task for her to do in life.

In 1867, her old mentor, Father Langevin, was named the first bishop of the diocese of Rimouski. In dire need of teachers for his new diocese, Bishop Langevin invited her on three occasions to come and help him set up an association of lay teachers. The first two times she declined his request, citing her ill-health. Then, at last, she relented, arriving in Rimouski on April 3, 1875, which was the first Saturday of the month, dedicated to Our Lady.

Élisabeth soon realized that a more stable way of life was necessary for this work and desired to devote herself to teaching as a religious rather than as a laywoman. At first the Bishop did not see that the foundation of a new religious community was practical for this apostolate. With a heavy heart, Élisabeth humbly accepted the Bishop's judgement, hoping that time and circumstances would show him that a new community was both possible and desirable. Suffering deep, inward pangs at this reversal, she redoubled her prayers to Our Lady of Sorrows, who, coupled with the Eucharist, provided her with strength during this dark night of the soul. At one point, on a gloomy winter's night in 1879, it seemed that the 13 members of the fledgling group of teachers would have to disband. They spent what was described as "a night of anguish" in resolute prayer before a statue of Our Lady in the chapel and, at the end, with the coming of dawn, they all agreed to remain faithful to their apostolate, come what may.

Not too long afterwards, in God's good time, came the turning point. Rethinking his earlier decision, the Bishop agreed, at long last, to the establishment of a new religious community. Our Lady had answered Élisabeth Turgeon's humble, persevering prayers. The new group was called The Sisters of The Little Schools, because their mission was to staff the poorest schools in the diocese.

On September 12, 1879, the Feast of the Holy Name of Mary, they pronounced their first vows, and Élisabeth became Sister Marie-Élisabeth. For their patron saint the Bishop gave them St. Francis of Assisi. As Mother Superior and foundress, Marie-Élisabeth formed her Sisters with great diligence in the most important Marian virtues, admonishing them, "Let us show great respect for our students. Mary is our model in the care she gave to the Child Jesus."

Some of her other prayers and sayings are no less elegantly simple and direct:

"Incomparable Mary, you who loved Jesus so much, help me that I may love him as you did without reservations and forever."

"I fervently pray that this good mother may be your counsel and your guide and sustain you in critical situations."

"I embrace you and place you in the arms of Mary, your true mother."

Quickly Mary, as she always does, brought Mother Marie-Élisabeth Turgeon to Jesus, fostering an intimate spiritual union between this holy foundress and her Divine Son. In March of 1881, not even two years after the establishment of her community, Mother Marie-Élisabeth began to suffer severe and repeated hemorrhaging. A few months later, just after midnight on August 17, she passed to her reward. On her deathbed she said to her nuns, "Always be loving towards one another. Love one another as Jesus loves you." Two days later, Bishop Langevin set himself the task of accompanying her last remains to their resting place. "I shall say the graveside prayers," he commented at the time, "I shall escort her to the cemetery. She was so very obedient that I owe her that."

On October 4, 1891, the name of her Congregation was changed to that of the Sisters of Our Lady of the Rosary. Shortly afterwards the Sisters adopted the motto, "All for Jesus through Mary". They have several houses in Canada, the United States, Honduras, Africa and Peru, their motherhouse being situated in Rimouski. On top of the motherhouse is a sign in lights, reading *Ave Maria*, a gentle reminder, to those passing by, of their loving Mother.

Marie-Josephte Fitzbach Roy (1806–1885) (Mother Marie of the Sacred Heart) Foundress, Servants of the Immaculate Heart of Mary

Marie-Josephte Fitzbach was born in St. Vallier de Bellechasse, Quebec, in 1806. Her father, Charles Fitzbach, died two years later; her mother remarried in 1812. While growing up, Marie-Josephte became deeply devoted to Our Lady. At 11, she made her First Holy Communion and then entered domestic service in Quebec City.

In 1828 Marie-Josephte married François-Xavier Roy, with whom she had three daughters, Séraphine, Célina and Clorinde. Five years later her husband died, followed by Clorinde at the age of 14 in 1846. In 1849 her other two daughters entered the Sisters of Charity of Quebec.

It was a lawyer, George Manly Muir, a member of the Society of St. Vincent de Paul, who alerted the Archbishop of Quebec to the pressing spiritual and material needs of prostitutes and other women who were being neglected by society. The Archbishop started looking for a woman to found an institute to care for these women and discovered the person he needed in Marie-Josephte.

On December 31 of 1849, taking the name Mother Marie of the Sacred Heart, she gave birth to a new religious family of nuns, calling them The Servants of the Immaculate Heart of Mary, Refuge of Sinners. Her first shelter for young women, which was placed under the protection of St. Mary Magdalen, was called the House of the Good Shepherd. Because of this, the nuns, while keeping their official name, became known popularly as the Sisters of the Good Shepherd. On February 2, 1856, the first seven members of the community made their religious vows before a painting of the Immaculate Conception, starting a custom that has been continued to the present. Two years later, again on February 2, they publicly consecrated their fledgling order to Our Lady. To this day all the members of the community consecrate themselves to the Immaculate Heart of Mary, praying to her for the conversion of sinners.

In every way, Mother Marie of the Sacred Heart took great pains to place her foundation in the hands of Our Lady, sure that she would quickly lead them all to the Heart of her Son, Jesus. In the community founded by Mother Marie, very special celebrations are held on the feasts of Our Lady, especially the feast of the Purification, February 2; the Feast of the Annunciation, March 25; the Feast of Our Lady of the Sacred Heart, May 31; and the Feast of the Immaculate Conception, December 8. Also, the third Sunday of every month is dedicated to the Holy Heart of Mary, while the month of May is entirely given over to Our Lady.

In the chapel of every house is found a cross flanked by the pictures of the Sacred Heart of Jesus and the Immaculate Heart of Mary. Also, each convent has its own *Pietà*. The constitutions of the order declare: "Daily recitation of the Rosary and of the Angelus remains for us Servants of the Immaculate Heart of Mary a privileged expression of our Marian devotion. Meditation on the mysteries of the Rosary will open our hearts more and more to the gift of contemplation."

In 1860 a convent of the sisters was established at Rivière-du-Loup. The immense chapel at the motherhouse in Quebec City was built in 1866 and dedicated to Mary Immaculate. By 1885 there were 14 other convents, the first foundation in the United States coming in 1882. In 1870 the community took charge of a reform school for troubled adolescents and then four years later started a "House of Mercy" for unwed mothers. When Quebec City was beset by fire in 1876, the preservation unscathed of the House of the Good Shepherd was attributed to an image of Our Lady of Purity that had been placed in one of the windows. In 1882 a special confraternity for the conversion of sinners was established at the motherhouse under the patronage of the Immaculate Heart of Mary and affiliated to the same confraternity in Rome.

Mother Marie, who died on September 1, 1885, was indeed the strong, faithful woman of the Scriptures, humble in her courage and goodness. The cause for her beatification was opened in the diocese of Quebec in 1990.

Venerable Alfred Pampalon (1867–1896) "The Hail Mary Saint"

Born on November 24, 1867 into a devoutly Christian family in Lévis, across the St. Lawrence River from Quebec City, Alfred lost his mother, Josephine, at the tender age of 5. The deep, unwavering faith of his parents was much like that of St. Thérèse of Lisieux's mother and father.

Madame Pampalon died giving birth to her twelfth baby, her oldest child being only 15 at the time. As she lay dying, she gathered her children around her and said to them with maternal tenderness, "My children, I love you much, but I must leave you. From now on, you will have no mother on earth, but I entrust you to a much better mother. I entrust you to Mary, your Mother in heaven. She will watch over each one of you."

A year after the death of his wife, Alfred's father, Antoine, thought it best to remarry, his second wife being Marguerite Phelan, an Irish woman who cherished Alfred as if he was her own child. Alfred returned the love and affection of his second mother with an open heart.

Alfred, who was good at sports and had a well-developed sense of humour, was taught at home by private tutors until the age of 9, when he continued his studies at Lévis College while living at home. Daily he would visit the parish church to pray. At first Alfred was not interested in becoming a priest, but a businessman, like his father, who built churches.

At 13 he was stricken with a serious illness, coming close to death. In the middle of this crisis, Alfred commended himself to Our Lady and promised God that, should he live, he would become a priest. When he was 17, he fell sick again with an inflammation of the lungs and renewed his promise to become a priest. Again he was cured. Following that, he made a pilgrimage on foot to the shrine of St. Anne de Beaupré in June of 1886. After praying to St. Anne, he asked to join the Redemptorist community there. A few weeks later, at the age of 18, he was sailing towards Belgium to begin his novitiate.

Above the door of the novitiate, in the town of St. Trond, there was a sign in Latin, *Mater Dei, sis intrandi janua coeli*, which means, "Mother of God, may you be the gateway by which we enter heaven." Here, on September 8, 1897, the feast of Our Lady's birthday, he pronounced his perpetual vows of poverty, chastity, and obedience as a Redemptorist. After this, there followed six years of philosophical and theological studies.

While he was not a brilliant student, his spiritual wisdom more than made up for any academic weaknesses. Good-natured and even-tempered, he was not averse to telling a joke and had a pleasant, easy-going air about him.

All through life he read and re-read St. Alphonsus Liguori's celebrated book, *The Glories of Mary*, and also *True Devotion to Mary*, by St. Louis Marie de Montfort. Resolutely, he promised Our Lady to become a saint.

He was ordained a priest on October 4, 1892, the third son in his family to receive the sacrament of Holy Orders, and was assigned for a time to give missions in Belgium. Although he was certainly not an eloquent preacher, his sincerity and holiness shone through his words, for his life was founded on prayer. Reciting many rosaries every day, he honoured Our Lady under several of her different titles: the Immaculate Conception, Our Lady of Perpetual Help, Our Lady of Sorrows, and Our Lady of Good Counsel.

Father Alfred would begin his day by prostrating himself in honour of Mary, showing by a physical sign that he entrusted all his waking actions to her. His every deed was lived between the space of two Hail Marys, for he made it his habit to say these matchless words of the angel's salutation to Our Lady three or four times an hour. Each night, he capped his day with a long prayer before the picture of Mary. Saturdays, he fasted and recited the canticles of St. Bonaventure in honour of the Mother of God.

All in all, he celebrated some 40 feasts of Our Lady during the year. Towards the end of his life, he proclaimed with a deep and astonishing burst of feeling: "I don't think that any man has loved a woman more than I have loved my good Mother."

His love for Jesus grew in proportion to his love for Mary, which was explicitly Trinitarian, as we see in this prayer that he composed to her: "Why don't I have for you all the love which God the Father has for you as his beloved daughter? All the love that God the Son has for you as his beloved mother? All the love which God the Holy Spirit has for you as his Blessed Spouse? O tender mother, how I wish to give you, who are the most tender of mothers, the most tender love of a son... ."

In 1895, very ill with tuberculosis, he was sent back to Canada after an absence of nine years and suffered much from the ravages of consumption. He staunchly refused any alleviation of his pain, including morphine. Father Alfred commented, "I am so happy to die in the house of St. Anne de Beaupré, near her privileged sanctuary. I am happy to die a Redemptorist... ."

On September 22 of the following year, he cried out, "The suffering is extreme. Good Virgin, open heaven. O Mary, come and get me. O, my good mother, come and get me. And yet, I still want to suffer for Jesus."

On September 26 he offered all his merits to Mary and asked her again to come for him. On September 27 he commented, "How good it is to pray to Mary and how happy one is at death. I have always loved her much." To a postulant he said by way of encouragement, "Love. Love Mary. This devotion will preserve your vocation."

On September 30, 1896 he declared, "I shall die today. Give me the picture of St. Joseph." This was at midnight. At 1:30 in the morning, all of a sudden, he sang the *Magnificat* from his chair. At 2 o'clock in the morning he asked for and received absolution. Then began the agony of his death. With his crucifix on his breast and the chaplet of Our Lady of Sorrows around his neck, he held in his hands the rules of the community, a Rosary, and pictures of Our Lady of Perpetual Help and St. Joseph. At his bedside, his brother Peter recited one Rosary after another. At 8:30 in the morning, Father Alfred suddenly opened his eyes and looked up to heaven. With a smile on his lips, as if experiencing a vision, he breathed his last. Our Lady herself had come to bring him home. He was 29 years old, his death occurring one year to the day before that of St. Thérèse of Lisieux.

Devotion to him began soon after his death and keeps growing. His intercession is considered to be especially effective in healing poor eyesight, as well as alcohol and drug addiction.

Father Alfred Pampalon was declared "Venerable" by Pope John-Paul II on May 14, 1991.

Blessed Louis-Zéphirin Moreau (1824-1901)

Bishop Moreau is the first Canadian-born bishop to have been declared "Blessed" by the Church. The fifth in a farming family of 13 children, he was born in Bécancour on the south shore of the St. Lawrence River across from Trois-Rivières on April 1, 1824. At 12 he began his primary school studies with a man named Jean Lacourse in his village. Sensing a call to the priesthood, he embarked on his classical studies three years later, in 1839, at the seminary in Nicolet, which was part of the Archdiocese of Quebec at the time. Then, not too long after he had started the theological part of his studies, he was sent home on account of frail health. Persevering in his attempt to become a priest, he was accepted as a seminarian by the saintly Bishop Bourget of Montreal, who placed him under the tutelage of his auxiliary bishop, John-Charles Prince. It was Bishop Prince who ordained him a priest in Montreal on December 19, 1846, when he was just 22 years old.

For the first five years of his priesthood, he exercised many functions: master of ceremonies and assistant at the cathedral, assistant secretary to the bishop, and chaplain to the poor in the Convent of Providence.

In 1852 the Diocese of St. Hyacinth was created, and Bishop Prince was appointed its first bishop. Making the

Immaculate Heart of Mary the principal patron of the new diocese, he invited Father Moreau to accompany him as his secretary and chancellor. There Father Moreau was to exercise many other responsibilities over the years: pastor of the cathedral, diocesan bursar, chaplain to nuns, vicar general and, finally, administrator of the diocese after the death of St. Hyacinth's third bishop, Bishop Charles Larocque in 1875.

Not only did Father Moreau serve three bishops with unflagging zeal and obedience, he was also keen to relieve the sufferings of the poor and sick and encouraged the rich to be generous in good works. "God knows the value of your almsgiving," he said, "and the God who rewards anyone who gives a glass of cool water in his name will not forget, in his goodness, to give you a hundredfold for your generosity accomplished with love." He became known as "the good Father Moreau", a man of deep faith, hope, and love, robed in an extraordinary gentleness and humility.

When, in 1876, aged 51, he was appointed fourth Bishop of St. Hyacinth, both clergy and laity acclaimed the pope's choice as an inspired one. Praying and working hard for priestly and religious vocations, he was concerned to ensure that his priests and nuns grew in holiness. When he took over the reins of the diocese, there were already some communities of Sisters there, including the Precious Blood Sisters and the Grey Nuns, whom he supported tirelessly. In addition to this, he brought in seven congregations of religious men and women, two of which he himself founded, the Sisters of St. Martha and the Sisters of St. Joseph.

As a bishop, he was faithful in visiting each parish of his diocese, so that, after 25 years in office, he had confirmed 48,000 of his flock. Approaching his role of shepherd with utmost seriousness, he was prompted to write many fine pastoral letters. As well, he encouraged the development of confraternities and pious associations. With a particular love for the children of his diocese, he desired to ensure them a solid,

Christian education. Being a man whose feet were firmly planted on the ground, he was no less concerned about the material needs of his people. Accordingly, he founded an association dedicated to St. Joseph, for instance, to help sick and infirm workers both spiritually and physically.

Reinforcing all this activity of his was the hour and a half he spent each day before the Blessed Sacrament. Bishop Moreau's main devotion was to the Sacred Heart of Jesus, his prayer life being immersed in it as a swimmer is immersed in the sea. In it he placed all his love and trust, all his deep desire to practise the virtues inherent in a Christian life.

Essentially, devotion to the Sacred Heart of Jesus was the means by which Bishop Moreau accomplished so much throughout his priestly and episcopal life. However, this devotion to the Sacred Heart was closely linked to his love for Our Lady, which was Christ-centred. Of her he said: "The Most Holy Virgin can do anything through the Heart of her Son."

"Let us piously venerate the Virgin Mary," he advised. "Love her tenderly. Honour her constantly by the practice of all the virtues that we admire in her, especially her virginal and angelic purity. Let us prepare ourselves to celebrate worthily the feasts which the Church has instituted in her honour and especially her Immaculate Conception. Let us glorify her to our very last breath by a profound attachment to and veneration of the dogma of her Immaculate Conception."

It is hardly surprising that he loved and recommended the Rosary as a powerful devotion:

"This moving prayer is so efficacious in touching the heart of Our Blessed and Heavenly Mother. Our Lady Mary is the dispenser of heaven's treasures. She loves us with a mother's heart. Let us present to her our requests with complete trust, with filial abandon. Let us love and help others to love Our Heavenly Mother. In return, she will cover us with her maternal protection during our time on earth and will introduce us into our home, the home of blessed immortality."

Even during Bishop Moreau's lifetime, many cures and other favours were attributed to his intercession. After his death on May 24, 1901, all the bishops of Quebec spoke out in praise of his undoubted holiness.

More recently, Father Peter Hussey of North Bay sought the intercession of Bishop Moreau, in the hope of obtaining a miraculous cure for Colleen O'Brien, an 8 year old girl dying of leukemia in North Bay Civic Hospital. Hanging a relic of the Bishop in her hospital room, Father Hussey prayed to him for a miracle and had others pray as well. Astonishingly, within a week, young Colleen was pronounced cured by the medical professionals who attended her. This was the miracle that allowed the Sacred Congregation for the Causes of Saints to recommend to Pope John Paul II that Bishop Moreau be declared blessed. His beatification took place on May 10, 1987.

Venerable Vital Grandin, O.M.I. (1829-1902) Apostle of the Northwest and First Bishop of St. Albert, Alberta

Vital Grandin, consecrated by his parents to the Blessed Virgin Mary even before his birth, was born on February 8, 1829 in a lovely stone house called "The Pelican", a wayside inn that had been built by his father, Jean, on the edge of the Sillé Forest in France. Vital was the ninth of 13 children in a poor family. Business was slow at "The Pelican", for Jean barred unsavoury customers from his inn and insisted that there be no drunkenness and misconduct.

Eventually, much to their regret, the family was forced to resettle in the small market town of Aron, where they struggled to make ends meet. The family's financial situation became even more precarious when their already meagre resources had to be stretched in order to support Jean, one of the older sons, who was studying for the priesthood. At age 10, Vital was sent to live with his Uncle Michael, tending his flocks and performing other chores. For Vital, a sensitive and highly affectionate child, leaving home was quite painful. Fortunately, he was able to return to his family not too long afterwards.

Nonetheless, there remained something sad about the boy, with his shy, retiring temperament. Inwardly, he was harbouring a dream, one that seemed to him quite hopeless, as he described it later in life:

"I had a secret desire to become a priest some day, but with my parents being so poor, I could see no way out."

Still, he kept praying to Our Lady. An exchange with his earthly mother confirmed his trust in Divine Providence:

"Would you not like to be a priest like Jean?" his mother asked.

"Yes, but we are too poor!" answered Vital.

"You are wrong," his mother replied, "We should always depend on God. Look at your brother... ."

Soon the obstacles in his way were lifted. It started when the assistant pastor at the parish undertook to teach him the rudiments of Latin. Then a certain Sister Anne-Marie, a Carmelite nun, arranged to pay for his board and lodging near the seminary, where he studied earnestly, with the help of his brother, Jean, and another seminarian. Soon, the Bishop's secretary, Father Sébaux, recognized his sterling qualities and arranged for him to enter the Précigné Seminary at the age of 17. A well-behaved, model student, he stayed there for four years, until 1850, impressing all those around him with his friendly temperament, which was still tinged by shyness. The only area of uncertainty was his frail health.

In 1850 he advanced to the Grand Seminary in le Mans. A year later, overwhelmed by the strong desire to become a missionary, he entered the Foreign Missions Seminary in Paris, enthusiastically looking forward to a life of sacrifice and possible martyrdom in the Far East. Whereas his mother, Marie, had died earlier during his seminary studies, his father, who was still alive, objected strenuously to his son becoming a missionary. To him Vital answered, "If God be everywhere, are we not bound to do our utmost to make him known and loved everywhere?"

Suddenly, after a mere few months, his superiors noticed a slight lisp that marred his speech and concluded he would never be able to learn an Asian language. Regretfully, they asked him to seek his vocation elsewhere. Vital clung desperately to the idea of becoming a missionary. His spiritual director encouraged him, saying, "I believe that you will be able to go to the foreign missions as a member of one of our religious congregations. Your health is not very good, but as St. Paul puts it, 'God has chosen the weak things of this world.'"

Then Vital was accepted by the Missionary Oblates of Mary Immaculate, Our Lady's own special congregation, founded in Marseilles, France, by St. Eugène de Mazenod only a few years earlier. After paying a visit to the sanctuary of Our Lady of Victory in Paris, Vital took the religious habit in their novitiate on December 28, 1851 and just over a year later, on January 1, 1853, pronounced his vows to become a full-fledged Oblate of Mary Immaculate.

Just before his priestly ordination he wrote home, "The day after tomorrow I am going into retreat. Can you guess why? Because I, your poor and unworthy Vital, am about to receive the greatest honour which God can confer upon a man. I am filled with fear and with joy. With fear because I am so unworthy. With joy because I know that God loves the weak and lowly." Ordained April 23, 1853 by Bishop Mazenod, he prepared to leave for Canada.

This time, his father's reaction was most encouraging: "I would rather see my sons sent to the hardest missions in the world, than have them remain in France and receive the highest honours which the government could bestow upon them."

In his first letter from Canada, dated June 28, 1854, Father Vital wrote to his brother, Father Jean:

"When the time came for me to leave, you were wonderful. You made my departure less sorrowful to our poor father and to the family... Together we knelt before the statue of our Blessed Mother and prayed for that strength which both of us so greatly needed. I can never forget your affection, your thoughtfulness as you took me aboard at Le Havre. I remember how you wept when I was ill. You took me away from the crowd aboard ship and into a church. In that church you took me to the small chapel, dedicated to Our Blessed Mother and there, on your knees you begged my blessing and then you blessed me and we embraced each other."

Reaching St. Boniface on the feast of All Souls, 1854, he set foot in a huge diocese which included the whole, vast frontier region of the Northwest. Here he studied several Indian languages and was appointed to the Nativity Mission, about 1,700 miles away, on the shores of Lake Athabasca.

At this, the most distant mission in the diocese, he began his apostolic career, an excruciatingly lonely life, subject to the severest mental and physical hardships in a rugged land beset by extremes of heat and cold, where he was forced to make long, exhausting journeys, oftentimes making his bed in the open air, a victim of hunger and thirst. In one of his letters, he did not shrink from sharing his inmost thoughts about this life and why he had chosen it:

"Humanly speaking I am not happy; but I submit myself to whatsoever my superior will command. I am happy since I am where the Lord wants me; and here, there is a possibility of making him known and loved."

Father Vital's mission was among the Montagnais tribe, where women were held in contempt and moral standards were very low. His open-handed goodness, marked by a spirit of unstinting self-sacrifice, quickly won the hardest of hearts. Both women and men flocked to him to be baptized. Many a time, groups of native people whom he had never met came to him, saying, "Our hearts are black with sin. Baptize us. Give us that water which makes our hearts clean."

Oftentimes, in the winter, he lived on frozen fish and weak tea, the temperature dipping as low as 45 degrees below zero. He ate a great deal of tough, leathery pemmican, and, during the warmer days, native people shared their meat with him. Surprisingly enough, his health had never been better.

When Father Grandin was only 28 years old, the Pope appointed him coadjutor, with right of succession, to Bishop Alexandre-Antonin Taché of the St. Boniface Diocese. The news came on him like a thunderbolt out of the blue. Strenuously Father Grandin protested his unworthiness, but to no avail. His superior, Bishop Mazenod, ordered him to France for his episcopal consecration. "Come at once," he wrote, "and please do not put off obeying my orders until after my death." Years later, Bishop Grandin reflected, "Of all the qualities required of a missionary bishop, I had only the desire to serve our dear God and to make him loved... and also a pair of long legs, well fitted to travel on snowshoes."

Submitting to the honour, he was consecrated in Marseilles on November 30, 1859 by Bishop Mazenod, his brother Jean and "good Father Sébaux" being among those present. He celebrated his first Pontifical Mass at the Oblate Shrine of "Notre Dame de la Garde", Our Lady who watches over the Marseilles Harbour. In the sanctuary were hung the coat of arms and motto he had chosen: a bent reed, the tip of which rested on the Cross, coupled with the words, "God has chosen the weak things of this world."

By 1861 the young bishop was back in northern Canada. Despite illness, he made the long, difficult journey to Ile à la Crosse, where he helped build the Grey Nuns' residence. In order to visit his fellow Oblate missionaries scattered in groups of twos and threes throughout the boundless northland, Bishop Grandin set off on an arduous journey which was to last three years. He longed to evangelize the native peoples all the way to the Arctic Ocean—a gruelling field of labour. At Our Lady of Good Hope Mission, for example, just below the Arctic Circle on the Mackenzie, one of the dedicated missionaries, Father Henri Grollier, was to waste away and die from lack of proper food.

The hardships that Bishop Grandin encountered while travelling were so great that many a time he came within a hair's breadth of suffering a violent death. He himself describes a typical winter's day vividly:

"One of the men goes ahead, axe in hand. I follow. Then come the dogs, drawing our provisions and theirs. And the second Indian trudges behind the sled, so as to push when necessary. My clothes are far from episcopal. They are not even clerical. Except for a flannel shirt, they are all made of leather. My trousers are moose-skin, my outer shirt is caribou-hide with the hair on the inside, and over it I wear a large moose-skin blouse. My cross and my episcopal ring hang from a cord around my neck. My finger would be frozen in no time, were I to wear my ring on it. From another cord hang two large sacks, made of white bear skin: they are my mitts and I have to keep my hands in them all the time. I wear a beaver skin hat, over which is a shawl to cover my neck, ears and parts of my face. All this peculiar head-dress is enveloped with a huge hood. Within half an hour of my putting it on, all the clothing near my face is covered with ice, due to my breathing. When there is too much ice, I change the position of the shawl. It was bitterly cold. My nose and eyes were three abundant sources which coated my shawl and face with ice. I wiped my eyes with my mitts and as the water penetrated to my hands and froze, the mitts became useless and my hands were numb with cold. As I pulled my weary legs along, I beat my hands against my sides in an effort to bring the blood back to my fingers, but I failed. I called to one of the men and showed him where to find another pair of mitts in my sack. I put them on and a larger pair over them. Had I to open the sack and look for the mitts myself, I should have frozen my hands. I finally succeeded in warming my hands, but by doing so, I froze my nose twice and my left cheek once."

At Providence Mission, he found that the native people were keeping away from him. Yearning to bring them the Good News, he began visiting their camps. "I went on to the last camp, praying that God, through the intercession of his most holy Mother, would put on my lips words that would draw them out of their apathy," he wrote. There, at the last camp, his prayers were answered: the people received him well. "You say that you love me," he told them. "Why, then, do you not come to see me? I love you and that is why I left my own beautiful country to live with you. Nine years ago today, I left my aged, white-haired father. I left him, although his heart bled and mine bled too, and all those who loved me wept to see me go. But when I wrote to my father and my friends and told them that the Indians at Athabaska and of Ile à la Crosse listened to me and live the life that takes us to heaven, my father and my friends were glad."

"I heard that you did not know how to go to heaven, so I left my good Indians to come to show you how to go to heaven. I came to you because you begged me to come. In order to remain with you, I suffered much. Look at my hands. What do those blisters and calluses tell you? The white men will soon come here to take your furs and when they go, I will have them take a letter to my old father. What can I now tell him to make his lonely heart happy? If I tell him that you do not care for religion and that you are wicked, it will make him die—and what excuse will you give to God when he judges you? Will you say that you did not know better? He will say, 'I sent my priest to tell you and you did not listen.'"

An old man arose and spoke for all. "It is true that we have said foolish things...," he said. "Our hearts are not as wicked as our words... We will now go to see you at your place and we will do what you say."

Bishop Grandin also had to contend with the hostility of some of the Protestant ministers and the Hudson Bay Company employees. Dire poverty dogged his every step. His clothes were worn and threadbare, and even the paper he needed for writing his letters was given to him in charity. In 1867 a fire destroyed the thriving mission at Ile à la Crosse. Immediately after this setback, he returned to France, where he spent months preaching on behalf of his northern missions, begging for help.

On September 22, 1871, when the new diocese of St. Albert was erected, covering all of Alberta and most of present-day Saskatchewan, Bishop Grandin was appointed its first Bishop. He and his 15 missionaries laboured tirelessly all over this vast territory, which was being inundated by great waves of European immigrants. Widespread traffic in liquor, with its attendant breakdown in morality, became a serious problem. Limited funds remained a pressing worry, forcing the bishop to take to the road and beg for the parishes, schools, and hospitals that were needed on this new frontier. Making matters even worse were the lack of cooperation and bigotry of some of the government officials.

Bishop Grandin was a deeply caring spiritual father to the native people in his flock, always anxious to protect them from troublemakers and other disruptive influences. When, in 1885, they got caught up in the rebellion, with all its bloodshed, it came to him as a cruel blow, well-nigh breaking his heart.

To help the Grey Nuns, who were already in the diocese, Bishop Grandin brought in the Faithful Companions of Jesus, as well as the Sisters of the Assumption and the Sisters of the Miséricorde. Also, since the promotion of vocations was another one of his pressing concerns, he established a minor seminary. He considered it one of the high-water marks of his episcopate when, on March 19, 1890, he ordained a Metis, Father Cunningham, to the priesthood. Because there were many Ukrainian immigrants in his flock too, he did all he could to provide them with priests who shared their language and rite.

With his health failing, worn out by age and years of unstinting apostolic labour, he was given a coadjutor bishop, Father Émile Légal, an Oblate, whom he himself consecrated on June 17, 1897. Early in 1902 he became more seriously ill and, as he lay bedridden, he embarked on the final leg of his life's journey, assisted by Bishop Légal, whose thoughts were, "We are witnessing the death of a Saint!" On June 3 of that year he passed on to the Father. In his last will, he began by paying homage to Our Lady, the spiritual Mother of the Oblates. Then he went on to thank his benefactors, adding, with characteristic selflessness that:

"If I happen to die while on the road, my wish is that in order to continue preaching the mystery of the Redemption even after my death, a large wooden cross be erected at the camp where I die. No expense is to be incurred to have my remains transferred; my body is to be buried at the foot of the cross."

As it happened, Bishop Grandin died in his own modest residence in St. Albert, surrounded by the love and affection of his religious family. The cause for his beatification was opened in 1937 and he was declared "Venerable" in 1966.

What incredible heroes, the Oblate Missionaries of the Northwest! Even Francis Parkman, with all his Protestant prejudices, could exclaim: "The 19th century produced no greater man than the Oblate missionary."

Humble and simple at all times, ever forgetful of self, Venerable Vital tried, like St. Paul, to make himself all things to all men, so as to gain all to Christ. This Francis Xavier of the Canadian Northwest did untold good by his untiring efforts and heroic example. Over the many years of his missionary apostolate, his journeys by canoe, snowshoes and dog sled took him a distance equivalent to eight or nine times the distance around the world. All this was done amidst the greatest hardships and sufferings by that same young man whose delicate health and weaknesses had been such that it seemed he could never become a priest. Instead, his prodigious missionary career lasted almost half a century.

In 1940, as a young priest in the Diocese of St. Albert, I was ministering to a sick old man. He was bitter about everything in the Church except Bishop Grandin. He admired and loved the man who had been his bishop 40 years before. As a seminarian, I read his biography and was present in St. Albert at the exhumation of his remains, praising God that he had been the founding bishop of my diocese.

Éléonore Potvin (1865-1903)
(Mother Marie-Zita of Jesus)
Foundress, The Servants of Jesus-Mary

The Servants of Jesus-Mary are a contemplative order of women dedicated to prayer and penance, especially for priests. Founded by Éléonore Potvin, a humble, hidden mystic who had a rich and fruitful relationship with Our Lady, they centre their spiritual life on Mary and the Eucharist. Pope John Paul II has commented on the intimate connection between

Our Lady and the Eucharist in his encyclical letter, *Mother of the Redeemer*:

"The piety of the Christian people has always very rightly sensed a *profound link* between devotion to the Blessed Virgin and worship of the Eucharist: this is a fact that can be seen in the liturgy of both the West and the East, in the traditions of the Religious Families, in the modern movements of spirituality, including those for youth, and in the pastoral practice of the Marian Shrines. *Mary guides the faithful to the Eucharist.*"*

Éléonore was born on January 4, 1865, in Angers, Quebec, which was part of the diocese of Ottawa. Her father died in 1875, and on June 29 of that same year she made her First Holy Communion at Our Lady of Grace Church in Hull. A few years later, in the same church, she was enrolled in the association called the Congregation of the Children of Mary. Even as a child, therefore, she had a strong devotion to Our Lady instilled in her by her mother. At home Éléonore would hum Marian hymns while she worked and set up little shrines to Mary with her friends. Endowed with a contemplative heart, she loved silence and recollected prayer. As she grew up, her passionate attachment to the Eucharist prompted her to walk six miles to daily Mass in any weather. After Mass she would spend hours in prayerful thanksgiving before returning home for her first meal of the day. In 1889 she tried her vocation as a cloistered nun at the convent of the Sisters of the Precious Blood in Toronto, but had to leave after a month on account of ill-health. The next year, aged 25, she became the housekeeper for her pastor, Father Alexis-Louis Mangin, in her home town of Masson. A wise, Marian priest, Father Masson was able to nurture her spiritual gifts. One of

---

* *Mother of the Redeemer, Redemptoris Mater: Encyclical Letter of the Supreme Pontiff, John Paul II*, Vatican Translation (Sherbrooke, QC: Éditions Paulines, 1987), pp. 81-82 (Art. 44).

his favorite sayings was, "The door to the heart of Jesus is Mary."

In her humility and littleness, Éléonore was truly one of the *anawim*, "the poor" so deeply loved by Yahweh. Taking particular pleasure in the Christmas scene of the Child-God and his Mother, she received most of her spiritual education and formation informally from the Holy Spirit by way of the Church's liturgy and her devotion to Mary.

In 1892 she assumed the habit of a Third Order Franciscan and took Sister Zita of Jesus as her name in religion. Later she would add the name of Mary. Meanwhile she lived on at the rectory like a religious, refusing to take a salary for her work. Her only disquiet came from her persistent desire to enter a cloister.

At the age of 28, for just over a year, she experienced several supernatural manifestations. The visions began on April 20, 1893, when she was in deep prayer. Our Lady appeared to her and said, "My daughter, wait." A few days later, Our Lady said, "My daughter, when I was on earth, I served my Son — and you, you serve a priest who is the representative of my Son." One day Jesus offered her the choice of two crowns, one of thorns and one of flowers. She opted for the crown of thorns, whereupon Jesus presented it to his Mother and then to Éléonore. With this, interior sufferings began to beset her, although she was aware all the while of Our Lady's maternal care. One day, when she was in greater distress than usual, Our Lady took her in her arms and pressed her to her heart.

On Christmas night, 1893, Our Lady appeared to her, nursing the Child Jesus at her breast. This phenomenon happened several times. Gradually, Éléonore came to understand that she too was to feed priests spiritually by the substance of her own being. Our Lady had said, "You will take care of my Son. You will take care of priests," which she understood to mean an apostolate of Eucharistic adoration and self-sacrifice for the sake of priests. Later, Our Lady nursing the Child became the symbol of the Servants of Jesus-Mary, who were to commission paintings and statues on the theme.

One day Jesus crucified appeared to her. There were rays emanating from his hands, his feet, and his side which, in turn, penetrated her hands, her feet, and her side. Thus, intensely united with the Lord, Éléonore was given the spiritual means to form the Servants of Jesus-Mary.

The last celestial manifestation took place April 27, 1894, the Feast of Our Lady of Good Counsel. In this vision, Our Lady appeared to her with the Child, whom she placed in Éléonore's arms. There Jesus said to her, "O you, my beloved, whom I have chosen for my spouse, you will always be in my heart. Since I have chosen you for my bride, I have also chosen you so that you would bring souls back to me. This you will do through suffering and humiliations, following my example. You will suffer all that to bring back souls to me."

With the help of Father Mangin, her spiritual director, she set in motion the plans for a new institute of cloistered, contemplative nuns, which was begun that year, on December 10, in nothing more than a stable. When she was appointed superior, Éléonore knelt before the statue of Our Lady of the Snows, the title that had been given to the nursing Madonna, and placed everything into Mary's hands saying:

"I, Sister Marie-Zita of Jesus, unworthy servant of Jesus and Mary, place my responsibilities at the feet of Mary Immaculate, our good Mother, praying and asking her to be our superior, since she is already our Mother. I promise to consider her in all things as being the true superior of the house, to consult her for everything and to make every effort to do the will of her divine Son in all things. I wish to be the servant of my Sisters. I wish to show my motherly affection as long as it pleases my superiors to leave me in charge of the community. I shall take the name of Mother-Servant."

The following year, on November 21, the "Little Stable" was transplanted to a convent in the town of Masson. In

December of 1898 the community moved once again to Aylmer in the province of Quebec, and from there, at last, on June 17, 1902, to Hull, across the river from Ottawa.

In time, Mother Marie-Zita came to embody Our Lady's virtues: her motherliness, full of tenderness and compassion, her discretion, her sensitivity, her goodness, her spirit of self-sacrifice, her mercy and forgiveness, and her serenity and joy. Anybody who came in contact with Mother Marie-Zita felt the supernatural air surrounding her. Like a little child, she turned to Mary with full trust, her love banishing all fear.

Throughout her busy day, she would constantly pray the Hail Mary. Whenever a crisis befell the community, she would gather all her Sisters together in the chapel, where, on their knees, they would recite the Rosary with arms lifted to heaven.

St. Louis de Montfort's treatise on *True Devotion to Mary* became the touchstone of the new Institute's approach to Mary. As a result, the community adopted the motto: "All to Jesus through Mary."

The Virgin Mother, true to her role of leading all people to her Son, gave her an insatiable longing for the Holy Eucharist. Her deep love for the Eucharist and the priesthood was like a great, consuming fire, fuelling the special charism of her sanctity. To suffer and work for the good of priests, who stand in the place of Christ, became the object of all her efforts. Our Lady and the Eucharist came to be the two poles of her life, which was cut short at the relatively young age of 38.

Having prayed to die on a Saturday, Our Lady's day, she was given her heart's desire, when the Queen of Heaven came to fetch her on the last Saturday of May, the 30th of the month, in 1903, during the recitation of the Angelus words, "Behold the handmaid of the Lord, be it done to me according to your Word."

On his historic visit to Canada in 1984, it was in the chapel of the Servants of Jesus-Mary in Hull, Quebec that Pope John Paul II celebrated Mass with the religious of the diocese.

Blessed Marie-Léonie Paradis (1840-1912) Foundress, The Little Sisters of The Holy Family

Blessed Marie-Léonie Paradis was born May 12, 1840 in the town of L'Acadie, Quebec, her baptismal name being Alodie. Her parents, Joseph and Émilie, were fervent Christians who taught Alodie to turn to Mary as to a mother.

At 14, Alodie joined the Marianists of the Holy Cross at Saint Laurent in Quebec. In 1857, just as she was finishing her novitiate, her father came to fetch her and take her home. "I threw myself down at the foot of the statue of Our Lady," she recounts, "and there, overcome with tears, I begged her to let me die rather than be dragged away from the hallowed walls of my novitiate... Then I suffered a hemorrhage in my lungs and began to cough up blood." Relenting, her father let her stay at the convent, so that on August 22 of the same year, despite her poor health, she pronounced her religious vows with the Marianists. This event filled her heart with boundless joy: "How will I ever be able to make a proper return for the happiness that I experienced on that day?"

As a nun she taught in Varennes, Saint Laurent, and Saint Martin de Laval and was also sent to New York in 1862 to run an orphanage. In 1870 she taught French and needle work at the Holy Cross Novitiate in Indiana. Four years later she arrived in Memramcook, New Brunswick, to be the director of formation for the young girls working at St. Joseph's College, administered by the Holy Cross Fathers.

In time, she became more and more attracted to the idea of establishing a community which would place itself at the service of colleges, seminaries, and bishops' residences. Several Acadian girls interested in the religious life gathered around her at Memramcook—the germ of a new apostolate. She started a handicraft centre in which to receive and train them, and by 1877 14 girls had joined her. Three years later, on May 31, 1880, the new community, having taken the Holy Family as its model, was approved by the Holy Cross Fathers.

For 20 years Mother Marie-Léonie unsuccessfully sought the approval of the bishop of St. John, New Brunswick for her new institute. At length, in 1895, the bishop of Sherbrooke, Quebec, Paul LaRocque, agreed to receive and endorse her community, which resulted in the motherhouse and the novitiate of the Little Sisters of the Holy Family being re-settled in his diocese. A year later, on January 24, 1896, he gave his formal seal of approval to the institute.

Many poor girls came to Blessed Marie-Léonie's door seeking religious life, but without an adequate education for it. Since the whole thrust of her charism was one of humble service, she was able to include these girls in her apostolate of providing domestic service for seminaries and colleges. In her wisdom, she gave them all a solid religious formation and trained them to be good cooks, laundresses, gardeners, etc.

Her humble nuns offered their lives of prayer and work for the sanctification of the priests and students they served. In pursuing this life of service—quite unglamorous and unfashionable today—they followed the scriptural example of Our Lady and the holy women who accompanied Jesus during his public ministry. Blessed Marie-Léonie had a high respect for the priesthood, with its awesome power to make Christ present in the flesh through the Eucharist. While she saw the priest as another Christ, she was by no means unaware of their faults and failings. Thus she admonished her nuns, "Don't talk about priests, for fear that you will not be able to say only good things about them. Double your courage and generosity in the service of God in the person of his ministers and their apostolates. Think of the favour God grants you in inviting you to co-operate in the beautiful work of education."

In addition to the main focus of her apostolate, she also opened her houses to the poor, visited the sick, and gave hospitality to nuns who had been expelled from France. "Our mission in the Church is to help priests on the temporal and spiritual levels," she explained, "but what God asks of us as a supreme witness is to love one another and to love everybody, not with any kind of love, but with all the love which God has. Everyday we must repeat without tiring that our principal work is love."

Blessed Marie-Léonie was deeply devoted to Our Lady, her attachment to the Mother of God being nurtured by her frequent meditation on the hidden mystery of the Holy Family living a simple life together in Nazareth. She considered Mary the ideal model for women in religious life.

Her intense Marian outlook was focussed especially on Our Lady of the Seven Sorrows and Our Lady of the Most Holy Rosary. Throughout her life, Blessed Marie-Léonie remained attached to the Marian custom known as the Forty Hours of Our Lady of Desolation, in which a member of the community would remain praying before the statue of Our Lady of Mercy from immediately after the Stations of the Cross on Good Friday until Easter morning.

The essence of Marian devotion that the foundress wanted to instil in every one of her Little Sisters of the Holy Family is symbolized by the Rosary, that most powerful of prayers. On the Feast of Our Lady of the Holy Rosary, October 7, she used to make several visits to her statue, bringing flowers each time. She was anxious that her Sisters should venerate all the mysteries of the Rosary, beginning with the Joyful Mysteries, which evoke the childhood years of Jesus, immersing the soul in the peaceful atmosphere of Nazareth.

For a Little Sister of the Holy Family, the Rosary was always to be ready to hand, her constant sacramental companion: at work in the kitchen, laundry, or sewing room, as well as on her way to and from the college, not to mention during walks in the garden. Work and prayer were to be intimately linked all day long in the lives of Blessed Marie-Léonie's spiritual daughters.

When she died May 3, 1912, there were thirty eight houses of her community established in Canada and the United States. Bishop Paul LaRocque, who had welcomed her into his diocese, had these words of praise for her: "She spent her whole life in giving. Her arms were always open and she wore her heart on her sleeve. She was joyful and often laughed, receiving everyone as if he or she were God himself. She was all heart."

Blessed Marie-Léonie was beatified in Montreal on September 11, 1984 by Pope John Paul II, during his historic visit to Canada.

Saints for the New Millennium

Blessed Frédéric Janssoone (1838-1916) "God's Travelling Salesman"

Blessed Frédéric Janssoone is certainly one of the more interesting and attractive figures in the annals of the Church in Canada, a man of irrepressible holiness, as can be sensed from the extraordinary radiance of his eyes and face in the photographs that survive of him.

Born November 19, 1838 at Ghyvelde in the north of France, young Frédéric lost his father at age 9. Afterwards, his schooling was cut short by his need to earn money for the support of his mother. For 6 years he took to the roads of France, going door to door with his linen samples and becoming a highly successful travelling salesman—a job perfectly fitted to his outgoing personality. When he was 25, God found another outlet for his talents. Like the little poor man of Assisi, Frédéric was overcome by a radical desire to give himself completely to God and joined the Franciscans, making his religious profession with them on July 18, 1865. Five years later, on August 17, 1870, he was ordained a priest.

In 1876, when he was 37, at his own request, Father Frédéric was sent to the Holy Land, where he was to be stationed for the next 12 years. This sojourn had a profound effect on his spirituality, grounding it quite literally in the life and times of the Lord. In this way he was able to swim upstream against some of the harmful undercurrents of thought that were circulating in his day and age. Among these were a spirit of Jansenism and a reactionary mistrust of Scripture. While those tainted by Jansenism stressed a fearful God of judgement, he constantly made reference to a good, loving God who forgives us our sins. While an exaggerated anti-Protestantism caused many Catholics to look on the Bible with suspicion and deterred them from reading it, he stressed the importance of meditation in depth on the Word of God, which he related to the mysteries of the Rosary.

His was a spirituality of flesh and blood, fully incarnational and Franciscan, utterly down to earth. To evangelize, he did not hesitate to use the mass media of his time: newspapers, books, and magazines. Because of his concern for social issues like agricultural production, one of his nicknames was "the beet-root priest". Also, he had an uncanny sense of how to get his message across to people, relying, for example, on his well-developed sense of humour.

In Palestine his abilities as a practical man of business stood him in good stead. One of his main tasks was to organize pilgrimages and re-establish devotion to the Holy Places. For example, he brought back the hallowed custom of making the Way of the Cross in the streets of Jerusalem. I was to find myself grateful to him for this years later, in 1950, when I was a pilgrim in the Holy Land and was privileged to walk in the footsteps of the suffering Lord through the streets of that ancient city. Also, Father Frédéric directed the construction of the church in Bethlehem and codified the arrangements which had been established between the Latins, the Greeks, and the Armenians for their use and support of the sanctuaries of Bethlehem and the Holy Sepulchre.

In 1881, as Assistant Superior of the Franciscan Custodians of the Sacred Places, Father Frédéric crossed the Atlantic to establish a Canadian Commissariat of the Holy Land and to seek funding for his apostolate. His charismatic demeanour and preaching made him an overnight sensation:

"His very appearance is a sermon. Upon seeing this friar standing on a stone, head bare, his face pale and coloured only by the effort of thinking, his body emaciated and seeming no longer to be of this world, while in his feverish and ecstatic eyes shines the light of another world, one feels that the supernatural is his element and that his life is Christ."*

That year he made his first visit to Cap-de-la-Madeleine and was delighted by the beauty of the sanctuary and its natural setting. There he met and encouraged the pastor, Father Luc Desilets, with whom he soon struck up a close friendship. When Father Frédéric fell dangerously ill in January, 1882, he spent almost four months in the rectory there convalescing, until he was suddenly called back to the Holy Land at the end of April. The time had not yet come for "God's travelling salesman" to take up the cause of Our Lady of the Cape.

That was to happen six years later, in 1888, when he was 49 years old. Just 14 days before the formal dedication of the shrine to Our Lady of the Rosary at Cap-de-la-Madeleine, he arrived back in Canada, where he was to remain until his death 28 years later. It was Father Frédéric himself who preached the moving sermon at the Mass of dedication on June 22, declaring prophetically that this would be a famous, much-visited shrine, attracting people from far and wide, even though its popularity was still merely local. The evening of that same day, he was one of three onlookers who witnessed the "Prodigy of the Eyes", during which Our Lady's statue came alive.

This was the third great watershed of Father Frédéric's life, after his "conversion" and his call to the Holy Land. The event of the statue's living eyes deepened his devotion to Our Lady and inflamed his soul, etching itself vividly on his memory, so that he was constantly making reference to it in the years that followed.

Father Duguay, Father Desilets' successor as director of the shrine, came to work closely with Father Frédéric and tells us of the Franciscan's heart-felt love for Our Lady:

"His confidence in Our Lady was like that of a child. He would speak of her with an extraordinary depth of feeling and

---

* James G. Shaw, *Our Lady of the Cape* (Montreal: Palm Publishers, 1954) 95.

admiration. In all of life's circumstances he would go to her with all the unselfconscious abandonment of a little child running to his mother. His confidence in her was so great that he did not hesitate to ask her for miracles, indeed, great miracles. Mary's goodness was his favourite subject. Whenever he spoke about her, tears would well up in his eyes. In the aftermath of the miracle, devotion to Our Lady took hold of his life completely. It made him a worker whose task, the task of promoting pilgrimages to Cap-de-la-Madeleine, demands our utmost respect and admiration."

Father Frédéric had always had a strong devotion to Our Lady, even before coming to the Cape. Many years later, for example, in 1891, he remarked that, "From my earliest childhood I have had a tender devotion to the Queen of Mount Carmel." An interesting preference, given his close association with the places of the Holy Land. Also, on his way to the Holy Land for the first time in 1876, he had stopped to visit the grotto of Our Lady at Lourdes, spending the night on her holy mountain.

After the "Prodigy of the Eyes" Father Frédéric took up permanent residence in Trois-Rivières and for the next fourteen years, until 1902, became the Cape's first Director of Pilgrimages, tirelessly promoting the shrine as only a master salesman could. He spread the word wherever he went, preaching powerfully, much loved by the crowds. His was a simple and spontaneous eloquence, not governed by ready-made rules of rhetoric. Once, for example, he was asked about the subject of his next sermon. "I don't know myself," he answered with disarming frankness, "I ask the Lord to put in my mouth the words of salvation that will best suit the needs of those who will hear me, and I speak as the Holy Spirit inspires me."

Slowly, the shrine became more and more popular, attracting ever greater numbers of pilgrims. While he was at the Cape, he would put himself entirely at the disposal of the pilgrims, hearing their confessions and explaining to them in conferences the mysteries of the Rosary, transporting them in spirit to the sacred places where these mysteries had taken place. Under the influence of Father Frédéric, a spiritual connection came to be established between the Holy Land and Our Lady of the Rosary at the Cape. This was further reinforced when he donated two relics from Palestine to the shrine and arranged for the erection, in 1900, of a wooden Way of the Cross there.

In 1892, he started putting out *The Annals of Our Lady of the Cape*, which are still being published today. When, on October 12, 1904, the statue of Our Lady of the Cape was solemnly crowned by order of Pope Pius X in the presence of most of the hierarchy of Canada, it was Father Frédéric who actually did the honours.

As can be imagined, the Rosary played an extremely important role in this holy Franciscan's Marian spirituality, which was clearly Christ-centred in a way that foreshadows the teachings of Vatican II. By means of the Rosary, he claimed, he could "take everyone with him on tour of the Holy Land," for he understood the Rosary biblically, as a meditation on the events of the Gospel in the company of Mary, the foremost disciple of Jesus.

More and more he began to think of Mary as a Mother of Compassion, stationed faithfully at the foot not only of her Son's Cross, but all the crosses we encounter as individuals on our life's journey. At one time, he even considered founding a community of lay Franciscans dedicated to adoring Our Lord on Calvary and placed under the special protection of Our Lady of the Seven Sorrows.

His heart being caught up by the theme of Our Lady's compassion, he had a special love for little children, as well as the poor, the ill, and the downtrodden. Father Prosper Cloutier relates this amazing little story about him:

"One day, I was taking him to see my cousin. On our way, we had to pass by the house of a sick man whose face had been eaten away by a cankerous growth. Father Frédéric asked if we could stop by and visit this man. When he entered the man's house, he went straight to his sick-bed. Kissing his sores, he blessed and consoled him. I found the whole thing deeply moving and edifying."

Widely known as "good Father Frédéric", he also had the gift of healing, attributing the cures to the Cross or Mary at the foot of the Cross.

Besides his work promoting Our Lady of the Cape, he preached numerous retreats and wrote many articles on the lives of Jesus, Mary, St. Ann, St. Joseph, St. Francis of Assisi and St. Anthony of Padua. Having a special regard for St. Joseph, he encouraged and supported Blessed Brother André in his efforts to honour the foster-father of Jesus. Also, he helped to re-establish the Franciscan Order in Quebec, after it had been nearly defunct there for 100 years. He travelled widely, moreover, to various parishes and dioceses in Quebec and New England to sell his writings, using the profits to help spread the Gospel.

Blessed Frédéric died in Montreal on August 4, 1916 from stomach cancer. His last words were, "Come, Lord Jesus! Don't delay!" He was beatified September 25, 1988 by Pope John Paul II.

During the process leading up to his beatification, one of his Franciscan confreres, who had lived with him for 12 years, recalled this remarkable little slip of a man (Blessed Frédéric was only five feet, two inches) and gave a glowing testimony to his virtue:

"The poem-prayer that I would apply to him and that suits him best, in my opinion, is the Beatitudes in the Sermon on the Mount. He lived out to the full this poetic passage from Scripture. It was the blazing light of his life. He was in possession of all the Beatitudes. Similarly, his devotion to Mary was his Magnificat."

Blessed Dina Bélanger (1897–1929)

The spiritual tone of Blessed Dina Bélanger's life was set early. Born in the Saint-Roch district of Quebec City in 1897 on April 30, the eve of Our Lady's month of May, Dina was baptized that same day, a Friday, and was given Margaret-Mary as her middle name. Here already Jesus and Mary were closely intertwined in her life, Friday being the day dedicated to the Sacred Heart of Jesus and St. Margaret-Mary being the saint who promoted this devotion. In her *Autobiography*, Blessed Dina herself remarks: "At the very dawn of my life, it seems, God in his goodness covered me with the protective mantle of the Virgin Mary."

Even as a young girl, taught by her parents, she saw herself as belonging to Jesus and his Mother. Instinctively she arrived at the conclusion that every baptized Christian, by being a member of Christ's mystical body, becomes a child of Mary, who gave Christ birth in Bethlehem and continues, until the consummation of the world, to give birth to him through his members.

At the age of six, Dina began her studies with the nuns of the Congregation of Notre Dame in Saint Roch, making her First Holy Communion when she was ten, on May 2, 1907. In her thirteenth year, a significant turning point of her life, she consecrated herself totally to Our Lady, according to the teachings of St. Louis de Montfort, achieving a wisdom beyond her years. Like that of St. Louis de Montfort, her consecration was Christ-centred:

"I surrendered myself wholly to the Blessed Virgin by means of the perfect devotion of Blessed Louis de Montfort. This entire relinquishing of self and possessions to the Queen of Heaven brought me great consolation and peace... It is she who leads us to Jesus. It is she whom we must allow to live in us in order that Christ may substitute himself in place of our nothingness. She is the surest path, the shortest and most perfect way to raise us to the infinite, to unite us to Uncreated Love."

In time Dina became an accomplished musician, studying in Quebec and New York City. Meanwhile, her desire to become a nun grew stronger, as did her attachment to Jesus and his Mother:

"Jesus and Mary are not separated in the history of the divine graces that I have constantly received. Jesus gave me, for guide and light, the Host and the Star. The Host was himself, the Star none other than his incomparable Mother."

At first she was uncertain which religious community she should join, until the voice of the Lord made it quite clear to her: "I want you at Jesus-Mary". In 1921, at 24, she entered the novitiate of the Sisters of Jesus-Mary in Sillery, Quebec and made her religious profession with them on August 15, 1923, taking the name, Mary Saint Cecilia of Rome. This community had been founded in France in 1818 for the apostolate of education by Blessed Claudine Thévenet.

The young nun soon fell ill. In her short life she stands as a model to all of us, especially young people, showing that God's love transfigures all our crosses. By offering herself, through Mary, to the heart of Jesus, whom she called "the life of my life", Dina invited the intimate presence of the Blessed Trinity into her soul. Entirely caught up in the desire to respond to the will of God, Dina may be likened to St. Thérèse of the Child Jesus, who left this world the year that Dina was born.

Dina, who wanted "to consume the whole world in love", has handed down her message to us with great, mystical clarity in her splendid *Autobiography*, which was begun in

March, 1924. In it she refers vividly to her relationship with Jesus and Mary:

"This morning I was closely united with Our Lord, but I still feared illusion. In my doubts and struggles, I addressed myself to Our Lady, saying, 'My good Mother, I beg of you, preserve me from illusion and do not permit me to place the least obstacle in the way of Jesus' action in me.' O joy; Jesus willed that his Blessed Mother should make answer: 'My child,' she said, 'As long as you remain closely united to me, you need not fear illusion. I shall preserve you always. So long as you seek God alone with an upright heart and with purity of intention, have no fear of contradictions. My Divine Son will make them turn to the glory of his Father, into the reign of his love.'

"The offering of Jesus to his divine Father has become a most urgent duty for me. I always make this offering in the hearts of Jesus and Mary and in the spirit of love. Thus, I understand that the Blessed Virgin offers Our Lord to the Eternal Father with one hand and, with the other, pours out upon souls the treasures of the heart of Jesus. I beg Our Lady to make this offering for me without interruption. Thus, when I look upon my Mother now, I always see her in the image I have just drawn. That is to say, in my place, offering unceasingly with one hand her divine Son to the Holy Trinity and as a result of this infinite offering, drawing from the Heart of Jesus and pouring upon souls with the other hand, inexhaustible treasures, according to the intentions and desires of this Sacred Heart.

"I found the motto for which I had sought so long and which corresponded to my every aspiration and summarized all my sentiments: 'Love, and let Jesus and Mary have their way.' This was an expression that satisfied me. The command to 'love' meant loving unto folly, even to martyrdom. 'Have their way' had the sense of perfect surrender, the self surrender that supposed alienation and destruction of myself. 'Let

Jesus have his way' meant that I should let the God of Love act freely. 'Let Mary have her way' was to entrust blindly to my Mother the task of realizing Jesus in me, cloaked and hidden by my outward being.

"All the graces of Paradise reach the earth by means of the Blessed Virgin. She is our all-merciful Mother who dispenses infinite riches. I will, then, be a little beggar of love on behalf of all souls for the greater glory of Our Father in Heaven. It is Our Lady who will distribute the wealth of the Heart of Jesus and, buried in the heart of Mary, I shall unceasingly beg their outpouring. Yes, in Heaven until the end of the world, I shall constantly beg for love.

"My task throughout eternity and until the end of the world is and will be to radiate through the most Holy Virgin the Heart of Jesus on all souls. The Heart of the Immaculate Virgin is an abyss of wonders. Enter this most pure sanctuary with respect and contemplate an incomparable masterpiece of purity, love, and every virtue. Mary is a mother. Her great desire is to clothe all her children with her own virtue for the glory of Jesus. You have entered into her heart. Do not leave it. Remain there and learn from her. Ask her to embellish your soul according to the divine ideal and in the heart of Mary you will soon come to know the heart of Jesus, the desires of the Eucharistic Heart of Jesus."

Jesus himself spoke to Dina about his Mother:

"'There is no invocation which better responds to the immense desire of my Eucharistic Heart to reign in souls than, "Eucharistic Heart of Jesus, may your kingdom come through the Immaculate Heart of Mary," and to my no less infinite desire to bestow graces on souls than, "Eucharistic Heart of Jesus, burning with love for us, fill our hearts with love for you." When you say "our hearts," have all souls, both present and future, in mind.'"

Blessed Dina's last motto was: "to love Jesus and Mary and make them loved." Her spiritual doctrine can be summarized simply: Surrender your all to the Heart of Mary, and she will quickly introduce you to the Heart of Jesus, who will find his pleasure in you and bring you in turn to the all-loving Heart of the Blessed Trinity, Father, Son, and Holy Spirit.

Blessed Dina Bélanger died September 4, 1929, at the age of 33, and was beatified by Pope John Paul II on March 23, 1993.

Adolphe Chatillon (1871-1929)

Adolphe Chatillon was born October 31, 1871 into a devoutly Christian family in the small town of Nicolet, Quebec, the fifth of nine children. Three of his sisters and one brother were taken from this world early, as was his mother, when she was just 37. Nine years old at the time of her passing, Adolphe was to harbour vivid memories of her: "What a good woman my mother was! She was a masterpiece of God's goodness. When I want to envision the tenderness of Our Lady, I recall my mother." Adolphe's father, who had spent two years in the Jesuit novitiate, was a strict disciplinarian with a passion for music, which he passed on to his son.

After his mother's death, young Adolphe was sent to a boarding school run by a friend of the family, Brother Theodulph, first at Baie-du-Febvre, then Yamachiche. At 13 he continued his education with the Brothers of the Christian Schools and came under the influence of a Brother with the delightful name of Symphorien-Louis, who confirmed and nurtured his devotion to Our Lady. Brother Symphorien-Louis, an artistic soul, was the author of *A Poetic Crown for the Mysteries of the Rosary**, a book of verse in honour of Our Lady that was highly acclaimed by well-known French writers of the day.

---

* original French title = *Couronne poétique des mystères du Rosaire*

Turning 16, Adolphe entered the novitiate of the Brothers and two years later began his long teaching career as Brother Théophanius-Léo. Adolphe was posted to the junior novitiate in Montreal, then in 1890 to the school at St. Jean d'Iberville. His next posting was to St. Jean-Baptiste School in Quebec City for four years. In 1895 he returned to the junior novitiate, where he became the vice-principal, acknowledged for his wisdom and compassion. Endowed as he was with musical talent, he took great pleasure in directing the choir, especially when they sang the praises of Our Lady. In later years his former students would vividly recall his infectious enthusiasm in promoting devotion to her:

"Whenever he announced, on the eve of Marian feasts, that there would be a catechetical instruction on Our Lady, we would burst out with applause. One evening, prompted by the theme of his talk to speak about heaven, he expressed himself with such passionate conviction and eloquence that we were all spellbound. I can still see him now, his eyes glowing, his face flushed, all animated as he tried to make us understand and indeed taste the happiness of the souls of the elect, their joy as they follow the Lamb wherever he goes, because they have remained pure. Never will I forget... ."

"Turn to Mary," he would say, following St. Bernard, "she will enlighten you, so that you may know the will of God for you. She shares in the light of Jesus Christ, her Son, who came into the world as light to everybody. She also is a true light which shines in the darkness. Pray to her often to enlighten your spirit and make it docile to truth."

When, in 1904, he was appointed principal of the school in Lachine, he prayed, "O Mary, divine Shepherdess, it is up to you to teach me the great and beautiful art of directing souls."

After a life-threatening illness in 1907, he was stationed at the novitiate as the Assistant Novice Master until 1912, when he in turn became the Novice Master. Immediately he entrusted the care of his novices to Mary, asking her to be the mistress of the novitiate.

Later he wrote, "Full Christianity is a personal union with our Lord, but we do not reach it without an unlimited devotion to the most holy Virgin. Mary is at the heart of Christianity, helping us to develop a fervent relationship with Christ."

In 1908, on November 21, the feast of the Presentation, Adolphe consecrated himself as Mary's child and slave according to the teachings of St. Louis de Montfort. He renewed it at every feast of Our Lady and wrote her name across the top of all his letters and papers. Out of conviction that sanctification came through Our Lady, he explained: "Always desire to please Our Lord, and to be more successful in this work, unite yourself to the most holy Virgin. It is the most direct way, the easiest means to arrive at a great perfection... How my heart desires that our good Mother be loved, honoured, and imitated more and more. How I wish I had the talent to make people love her and pray to her." Since there was a painting of "Our Lady of the Interior Life" at the novitiate, he encouraged his novices to turn to Mary under this title. Also, he had a grotto to Our Lady of Lourdes built in the gardens there.

To his brother Robert, an Oblate missionary in Mexico, he wrote in 1914, during World War I: "Let us throw ourselves into the hands of Providence... and take refuge in our beloved Mother for the past, the present and the future. In her and through her, peace will come."

From 1923 until his death in 1929 he was an international adviser for the training and formation of the Brothers in his order. In this role he visited the novitiate and scholasticates in Montreal, Quebec, Toronto, New York, Baltimore, St. Louis, San Francisco, New Orleans and Santa Fe. Also, he made two trips to Europe, first to participate in a General Chapter of the Brothers and then to elect a new Superior General. These travels gave him an opportunity to share his love of Our Lady with hundreds of brothers and students. Audiences found him a captivating speaker, with clearly expressed ideas that drove right to the heart of his subject matter.

In 1928 he was struck down by cancer. In his last moments he called on Mary, "Immaculate Heart of Mary, pray for me. O Mary conceived without sin, pray for us. Good Mother, adorn my heart, enlarge it so that I may love Jesus better. Jesus, my heart is not worthy of you. Purify it. Mother, help me to purify my heart and make it worthy of heaven." Adolphe Chatillon died on Sunday, April 28, 1929, his last words, like those of the Little Flower, being, "I too will spend my heaven doing good upon earth."

The cause for the beatification of this Brother of the Christian Schools was introduced in Rome a few years ago.

Gérard Raymond (1912-1932)

I first heard of Gérard Raymond while I was in college in the 1930's. This remarkable young man was a philosophy student at the Seminary in Quebec City, six or seven weeks shy of his 20th birthday when he died, full of a wisdom beyond his years.

Even before he was born, while still in his mother's womb, Gérard had been consecrated to Our Lady. After his birth on August 20, 1912, the feast of St. Bernard, he was dedicated to Our Lady yet again. To his mother, who first instilled in him a devotion to Our Lady, he gives a heart-felt tribute, "After God, it is to her that I owe all that I possess of piety and of virtue. It is thanks to her that I have kept my innocence."

Of Our Lady, who was the keystone in the early flowering of his holiness, he talks in a similar vein of gratitude: "Yes, O Mary, it is you who, with God, have given me the strength to do all that I have accomplished of good until now. The victories I have won, I owe to you. It is to you that I owe the person that I am now. O my good mother, thank you... Hide me under your mantle in silence, far from the noises of earth. O Mary, pray for me."

On the face of it, his outward development was ordinary for a boy of his time and place, brought up in a traditional Christian culture, with parents who practised their faith and communicated it to their children. What made him exceptional amid his everyday duties and routines was the way he interiorized and lived what had been taught him. Like many a boy of his generation, Gérard attended Mass daily and was faithful to the Rosary, but much was happening in his soul that could not be seen. This was revealed to the world only after his death, when his journals were discovered, showing that he had enjoyed a rich outpouring of graces through the mediation of Our Lady.

Because of the briefness of his life, Gérard Raymond has been compared to St. Stanislas Kostka, who died at the age of 18, and to St. Louis Gonzaga, who died at 23. In bygone days both these saints and even Gérard were commonly presented as Christian models to young people. Today, on the other hand, their lives seem remote from our concerns. To read the life of Gérard is to breathe the air of another world, so far removed from ours that it seems like a dream. The modern reader is apt to dismiss the story of his witness as the product of another age no longer relevant to our own. If, though, we are honest, we must recognize our own cultural conditioning and ask whether this is a proper response in the light of Gospel truth. Because the Evil One is a wily tempter, we need to be on guard against conceding too much to the neo-pagan culture all around us. It is all too easy to doubt the power of grace in the life of every baptized Christian and give in to the prevailing spirit of our age. If the early Christians had clung to the moral standards and outlook of their times, they would never have converted pagan Rome. Like them, we must stand outside the culture of death and bring to it the life-giving message of the Gospel.

No doubt, where Gérard Raymond goes most against the modern grain is in his wise appreciation of the indispensable importance of chastity:

"I believe that I have been called to religious life... The greatest obstacle to the priesthood is impurity. I am pure and want to remain so. Holy Virgin, pray for me." Among the resolutions he made after a retreat in 1929 was: "To cultivate my ideal of the priesthood. To enter into valiant combat in the company of Jesus and Mary. And always to remain chaste."

In a journal entry for June of 1931 he relates: "I renew today the vow I have already made. I consecrate myself to chastity, virginity, and absolute purity for all of my holidays. With the grace of God, I will avoid any deliberate act which could tarnish this holy virtue. I pray to you, O Mary, my good mother, to offer this vow to your divine Son, so that it may reach the throne of God. Protect me, help me, O Mary."

Gérard's balanced human qualities are evident in his journals, which cover every facet of his daily life: the books he read, the essays he wrote, the sermons he heard, etc. In this personal record, which he started when he was 15, he comes across as a young man who was full of life and ambition, without false modesty or morbid introspection, more than ready to acknowledge his successes: "Last year I won many first prizes. God has given me talents and I want to make them bear fruit for his glory."

Endowed with a strong will and high ideals, he wanted to become a missionary some day. One All Saints Day, he added quite simply, "I also have resolved to become a true saint."

During his annual retreat in 1928, he noted, "My vacations have been excellent. Daily Mass and Communion, the Rosary." On February 3, 1929, he reported in his journal:

"This morning I was received as a member of Our Lady's Sodality. Now I am consecrated to Mary forever. I have chosen her as my patroness, my mother. I have promised to be always faithful to her. May I always fulfill these promises perfectly. I have sworn to it. It is for life. I belong to Mary."

The same year, on May 16, just before the Marian Congress of Quebec, he made a pilgrimage to the Chapel of Our Lady of Victory, summarizing the sermon he heard there:

"Mary is Our Lady of Grace because more than any other creature, she is full of grace. Because she has merited grace, because she is the treasurer of grace, her intercession is all powerful. I will try to imitate Mary, taking her as my model for doing my duty, doing perfectly little things. She will be my ideal and I will trust her, assured of her powerful intercession. Mary, O my mother, bless me, help me."

On June 21, 1931, he confided to his journal, "I went to confession after a meditation on death. I did not find grave sins in my past life, either materially or formally. Jesus, may I never deliberately offend you, even venially... My prayer is that you keep me this way for the rest of my life."

Gérard Raymond died of tuberculosis on July 5, 1932, offering up the last months of his illness as a sacrifice for the good of his own soul and the conversion of sinners. The cause for his beatification has been introduced in Rome.

Paul-Émile Martel (1915-1933) (Brother Denis)

Although he died when he was only 17, Paul-Émile Martel lived long enough to grow into a mature Christian. In his childhood, at Pont Rouge and Saint-François d'Assise de Québec, his faith was nurtured by a solidly Christian family life. Like many Québecois families in the 1920s, the Martels were devout in the practice of their faith. Reciting the Rosary and other family prayers was a normal, everyday part of their lives.

At an early age Paul-Émile felt drawn to join the Brothers of the Sacred Heart in Arthabaska. Overcoming the misgivings of his parents, who thought he was too young, he became a student boarder with the Brothers, determined even then to leave all worldly ambition behind in order to follow Christ. During this time, when he was only 15 years old, his mother died. While she was ill, he wrote to his family, "We made a novena to the most Blessed Virgin, but we still have not obtained Mama's healing. We must not be discouraged. Jesus is the Master and he alone knows what we all need. Therefore, have no fear, for Jesus loves us too much to abandon us." This profound statement, coming as it does from a boy scarcely out of his early teens, illustrates one of the most important features of Paul-Émile's spirituality: his extraordinary attitude of abandonment to the will of God.

At the beginning of his novitiate, Paul-Émile received the habit of a Brother and the new name Denis. Having lost his earthly mother, he attached himself all the more to our Blessed Mother, his spiritual journals being full of prayers and petitions to her. Every morning he prayed before the statue of Our Lady of the Sacred Heart.

For him, Mary was always the intermediary, leading him closer and closer to the heart of Jesus: "O Mary, you who know how difficult it is for me to develop an interior life... May I not be a sterile tree in the garden of the Sacred Heart of Jesus, your Divine Son." Discovering God's intimate love for him, Paul-Émile became a true Brother of the Sacred Heart of Jesus through the Heart of Mary. On June 6, 1932, he prayed: "Mother Mary, I want to draw love for the Heart of Jesus from you."

Paul-Émile also came to have a great devotion to St. Thérèse of Liseux, the Little Flower, referring to her in a journal entry for October 3, 1931: "Today and for several days now, I experience great joy at the thought that I too, if I want to, can become a saint in the manner of Thérèse of the Child Jesus." It was St. Thérèse who had pointed to Our Lady as her model and prayed to her: "O Mary, you have made the narrow road to heaven visible by always practising the most humble virtues. Beside you, O Mary, I love to remain small." Like St. Thérèse, Paul-Émile wanted to remain humble and hidden in the Heart of Jesus through Our Lady, which prompted him to remark: "I will especially try to imitate Mary in her immense purity as well as her humility and her love of the hidden life."

Paul-Émile often renewed his consecration to his heavenly Mother. On May 1, 1932, for example, he wrote, "I ask you, O sweet Madonna, to be the guardian of my holy vocation, of that priceless treasure which I have received from the Heart of Jesus himself. I know, O good mother, that if you deign to guard it, I will be certain to die as a true Brother of the Sacred Heart, after having lived as a saint."

At the age of 16 he prayed that at his death he would receive the last Sacraments and the assistance of Mary: "O Divine Heart of Jesus, O Immaculate Heart of Mary, I beg of you, because of your love for me, allow me to die as a holy religious after having received the holy Sacrament of Extreme Unction and the holy Viaticum." It was as if he had had a premonition of his last illness. Soon afterwards he was stricken with an acute kidney infection and taken to the hospital. He was to leave it in a coffin.

On the eve of his death, he asked his confreres to "pray for me, that my last act may be an act of perfect love."

His was a short life, like that of St. Thérèse, but one filled to the brim with the loving praise of God for his infinite goodness. Like the Little Flower and the *anawim* of Scripture, he was humble and hidden, exceptional not in spectacular, outward deeds, but in his unconditional love of God and total trust in him. Having understood and accepted the role of

Mary in the life of a Christian, he was led by her to Jesus, who "did marvels" for him.

The cause for the beatification of Paul-Émile Martel has been opened in the Diocese of Nicolet.

Bishop François-Xavier Ross (1869-1945)

François-Xavier Ross, twelfth in a family of fourteen children, was born on March 7, 1869 in the mission parish of Grosses-Roches, part of the diocese of Rimouski. The son of Joseph Ross, a settler who had married Marcelline Gendron twenty years earlier, he considered his mother a saint. It was she who laid the earthly foundations of his spiritual development. Under her guiding influence, a deep attachment to Our Lady was woven into the fabric of his heart and soul.

Beginning in the year of François-Xavier's birth, religious services were held in the Ross family home. Confirmed on July 10, 1882, the young François-Xavier thrived in a faith-filled household and grew to love the land, the sea, and the forest, harbouring a lifelong nostalgia for the place of his birth.

In 1882 François-Xavier embarked on his classical studies in Havre-Saint-Pierre under Bishop François-Xavier Bossé, who had established a minor seminary in his rectory. The following year François-Xavier left for the Minor Seminary of Quebec, where he remained for eight years. Then, after one year in Quebec's Grand Seminary, he was asked by Bishop André-Albert Blais to come back to Rimouski to teach his seminarians arithmetic and algebra, while continuing his own theological studies. In 1892, when only a subdeacon, he was named secretary to the bishop. Ordained a priest on May 19, 1894, he remained the bishop's secretary for two more years. From 1896 to 1898 he was a missionary in Matapedia, following which he became the founding pastor of l'Anse-aux-Gascons, building a church and rectory. In 1901 he was named pastor of the church in St-Louis-du-Ha-Ha, leaving there in 1904 to go to Rome for a doctorate in Canon Law, which he obtained in 1906.

On his return from Rome, Father Ross was named Principal of Rimouski's normal school. Until 1923 he was the guiding light of the normal school, even while he filled the important role of vicar general for the diocese.

On May 1, 1923, he was given episcopal consecration and installed as the first bishop of Gaspé two days later. In all he was to do as founder of this diocese, he stayed close to Our Lady, placing all his undertakings under her protection.

A month after his installation he invited the Ursulines of Quebec to establish a monastery in Gaspé, which he solemnly dedicated to Our Lady of the Assumption on August 5, 1925, the Feast of Our Lady of the Snows. From this monastery the Ursulines administered a normal school, a boarding school for girls, and school of home economics.

On October 7, 1923 Bishop Ross announced his plans to build a seminary, placing the whole project under the patronage of Mary Immaculate. In its cornerstone, which he blessed June 7, 1925, he placed two medals: one with the Sacred and Immaculate Hearts and the other bearing an image of Our Lady of Protection. On September 8 of the following year, just days before the seminary, which was run by the Jesuits, first opened its doors with 69 pupils, it was consecrated to Christ the King and placed under the protection of Mary, Mediatrix of all Graces.

Shortly afterwards, he announced the foundation of a diocesan hospital, entrusting it to the Hospitaller Nuns of Quebec. On December 8, 1926 he placed their monastery and novitiate under the patronage of Our Lady of the Snows.

October of 1928 witnessed an extraordinary event in Bishop Ross' diocese: the birth of the Missionary Sisters of Christ the King, a new religious community, charged with the special mission of spreading the kingship of Christ in pagan countries through devotion to Mary Mediatrix.

The bishop encouraged all his parishes to establish the Society of the Children of Mary and numerous other confraternities and associations. In 1925 he obtained special permission from the Holy See for his diocese to celebrate the office and votive Mass of Mary Mediatrix of all Graces on May 31. "Mary deserved to be consecrated by the unity of the Divine Plan as a secondary mediatrix or distributor of the graces accorded by her Son for our redemption," he wrote. "What has prompted us to ask for this feast for our diocese is a desire to render a tribute of gratitude to the Holy Mother of God, who has been for us a channel of graces without number. I also desire that we should have a growing confidence in her powerful mediation, which we need so desperately for the many, overwhelming tasks that we have yet to accomplish."

Bishop Ross was invited to give a talk at the first Marian Congress of Quebec, held from June 12 to 16, 1929, at which he pointed out eloquently that devotion to Our Lady is not merely another devotion among many: "...but it is of the very essence of Christianity. Its roots are found in those fundamental dogmas on which revelation has laid the foundations of the Incarnation of the Son of God and the Redemption of the world. By one and the same divine decree, God ordained the Incarnation of his Son and the woman from whom he received his humanity, which had to be sacrificed for the Redemption of the world. Thus, Mary enters into the economy of the divine plan of Redemption. After having paid the debt of humanity by suffering and rising again, our Redeemer wanted to make all men holy by allowing them to join the family of God. He himself remains the first-born of many brothers and sisters who by adoption become children of God made in his very image. Because these children need a mother—inasmuch as the supernatural order of things is similar to the natural order—they were given the Mother of God as mother, becoming siblings of Jesus, who is their first-born elder brother. It was fitting that Mary should become the Mother of all men. In this way she enters once more into the economy of the divine plan of Redemption. In this divine plan, Mary occupies an incomparable place of honour, one which puts her above all creatures and associates her intimately with our Redemption."

At the second Marian Congress of Quebec, held two years later, from September 17 to 20, 1931, Bishop Ross gave yet another talk on the role of Our Lady.

In October of 1942 Bishop Ross had a shrine built in his diocese to Our Lady of Sorrows, explaining:

"Wherever this devotion is established, we notice a growth in love for Mary and love for God. My dearest wish is that pilgrimages be merely the first manifestations of a devotion which I hope will penetrate the whole diocese and even further."

On April 13, 1945, a few months before his death, Bishop Ross urged his priests and people to consecrate themselves to the Immaculate Heart of Mary on the first Sunday of May. In this letter he recalled that Pope Pius XII had consecrated the human race to the Immaculate Heart of Mary and had endorsed the message of Fatima, which beckons modern man back to Christ. Encouraging the practice of observing five consecutive first Saturdays of the month, he repeated the words of Cardinal Carejeira, the Patriarch of Lisbon: "The world is embarking on a new era, that of the Immaculate Heart of Mary." Emphasizing the recitation of the Rosary, he pointed out that Pope Leo XIII alone had written 12 encyclicals on this subject. Popes Benedict XV, Pius X, Pius XI, and Pius XII, he remarked, were all of the same mind in attributing great importance to the intercession of Our Lady and the recitation of the Rosary. The Bishop then gave an overview of the unique role played by Our Lady in the history of Catholic spirituality and concluded his letter by insisting that all the churches in the diocese have Marian devotions in May and that all parishes, institutions, and individuals renew their consecration to her Immaculate Heart.

Beginning in 1923, Bishop Ross received many honourary degrees and awards. In spite of this, he remained an ordinary, unaffected man who had a tender, lifelong love for the Mother of God. An exemplary bishop, he died at the Hôtel-Dieu of Quebec on July 5, 1945, and was buried in the Ursuline Cemetery there.

Father Marie-Eugène Prévost (1860–1946) Founder, Priestly Fraternity and Oblates of Bethany

Eugène Prévost, the founder of two religious communities, was born August 24, 1860 in St. Jerome, Quebec and baptized the next day. His parents, Dr. Jules Prévost and his wife Hedwidge, gave their son a solid Christian upbringing in a loving family. On July 6, 1869 Eugène made his First Communion, describing it later as "one of the great graces that had specially marked my life with a stamp of happiness". Five years later, in 1874, he was confirmed.

At 13 he was sent to school in Montreal with the Sulpicians, after which he was enrolled in the junior college at Sainte-Thérèse, where he proved to be an unruly, rebellious student. While en route back to his classes after holidays early in 1877, he almost died from exposure to the bitter cold and was taken home to convalesce. When it came time to go back to school, Eugène wanted to drop out. At the insistence of his parents, he returned to the junior college. Still sidelined as an invalid, he took refuge before the Blessed Sacrament, siezing the opportunity to reflect on his life. At the age of 17 his heart was touched forever, causing him to exclaim with joy: "O my God, I thank you for having converted me through your Sacrament of fire".

Wasting no time, he consecrated himself to Our Lady: "O Mary, I give myself to you forever. I choose you for my mother and my advocate before God. Give me your love and the love of your Son. O Mary, may I love you all the days of my life... May I now abandon worldly things and consecrate myself to your glory and the glory of Jesus, your Divine Son."

Feeling a call to the priesthood, he entered the Seminary of Philosophy in Montreal and was clothed with a soutane in September of 1879. Then, having heard about the Congregation of the Blessed Sacrament, which had been founded in 1856 by St. Peter Julian Eymard, Eugène crossed the Atlantic in the summer of 1881 to join the order in Brussels, making his profession two years later on September 29, 1883. On the eve of his priestly ordination on June 4, 1887, in Rome, he turned to Our Lady, asking her poignantly to be his "Mama": "O Mary, gentle and tenderly loved Mother, lead me, assist me, protect me. You know how much my heart is filled with love for you and how determined I am never to be separated from you. I have chosen you, so that you might make me a holy priest. Tomorrow be my tender Mother. Present me to Jesus, unite me to him. Answer Jesus for me, assuring him of my fidelity, and always, always, be my loving Mama".

The next day, he had a mystical experience, a sense that Our Lady was standing by him during the ordination ceremony, which was a sign that she had recognized him as a priest, as "another Christ": "I had a strong feeling that Mary was present with me at my right side. That tender Mother of mine was there with me for the whole ceremony. I had a vivid appreciation of the new, unbreakable bonds that were being forged, linking her with my priestly soul forever."

After ordination, he was put in charge of the Priests' Eucharistic League in Paris for 11 years, where he fostered devotion to the Blessed Sacrament. With other Blessed Sacrament Fathers, he prepared the national pilgrimage to Lourdes on August 15, 1890.

The spirituality of Father Prévost was centred on the Eucharist and Mary. It is Our Lady, he realized, who draws us to the Eucharist, teaching us how to love and serve Jesus in the Blessed Sacrament. In a spirit of devotion to Our Lady, he added Marie to his first name and also to his pen name, Marie-Eugène of the Cross.

St. Peter Julian Eymard had envisioned founding two religious orders with close ties to his Blessed Sacrament Fathers. One of these, a contemplative order of women, was established as the Servants of the Blessed Sacrament, while the other, conceived as a more active community of men, was never realized in St. Peter Julian's lifetime. It was left to Father Prévost to nurture the seed that the founder of his order had planted.

Through his many contacts with priests, their pressing needs were brought home to him as the focus for a new apostolate. One day, while he was in prayer before the Blessed Sacrament, he was given an illuminating grace, which directed him to leave his order and strike out on his own. This was a critical crossroads in Father Prévost's life, similar to that experienced by St. Ignatius of Loyola at Manresa. On August 1, 1900 he made the greatest sacrifice of his life, as he signed the indult dispensing him from his vows as a religious.

Now he set to work establishing an order of women called the Oblates of Bethany and an order of men known as the Priestly Fraternity, both of them dedicated to the service of Christ the High Priest through aid to his priests and Eucharistic adoration, anchored in love for Our Lady. By the time of his death on August 1, 1946, at La Beuvrière, near Angers, in France, there were 10 houses of the Fraternity and two of the Oblates. Since then the cause for his beatification has been opened. A prolific and talented writer, he left behind a large body of writings that testify to his wisdom and holiness.

Following in the footsteps of their founder, both congregations have a special devotion to Mary Immaculate, renewing their consecration to her every year, on December 8. Also, they pray the Rosary daily and take special care to celebrate the liturgical feasts of Our Lady. At Father Prévost's urging, they "love Mary as children love their mother, doing everything in union with her, in a great spirit of love and abandonment."

Father Prévost encouraged his spiritual sons and daughters to be profoundly Marian: "Go to Jesus through Mary and learn from her adoration in spirit and in truth, as well as zeal for Jesus in priestly souls."

He advised them to grow in love for Jesus and his Mother by acknowledging their mutual relationship: "To adore and love the Sovereign Priest, Jesus, in the Blessed Sacrament, borrow the heart of Mary. To exalt and love Mary, borrow the heart of Jesus... ."

The love of Jesus, he explains, entails love of his Mother:

"If you wish to know the degree of your love of Mary, calculate the measure of that which you bear towards Jesus. When you think about Jesus, everything speaks to you of Mary and you cannot think of the Son without thinking of the Mother. You cannot be aglow with love for Jesus without, at the same time, loving her through whom he was given to you."

Of Our Lady's inexpressibly close ties to her incarnate Son, he writes eloquently:

"Without her, you would not have had Jesus. Had she not been his Mother, you would never have known her Divine Son. Had she not given him life, you would never have seen Jesus climbing Calvary and offering himself as a sacrifice for your salvation. If she had not supplied the flesh and blood of God made man, you would never have known the inexpressible sweetness of the Blessed Sacrament and the Communions in which you are given the flesh of God... ."

"This Jesus whom I adore in the Host and upon whom I feed, was prepared for me by you, and from him I learn how dazzling is your purity and how immense is your love. You live in Jesus. You adore him and you love him in all his mysteries. You recall his whole mortal life and follow him step by step.

"How beautiful it is to think of Jesus being born, living his earthly life, suffering and dying like ourselves, but everywhere you meet him, you find Mary beside him. At Bethlehem. In Egypt. At Nazareth. On the road to Galilee and Judea. On Calvary and at the foot of the Cross. Jesus is never alone. Mary is there to live, suffer and die (mystically) with him.

"If therefore Jesus did not will to be separated from his Mother in life and in death, how could you love him and all his mysteries, without at the same time loving her, who was so closely associated with him? One day you will contemplate Jesus and the splendour of his glory, and loving him with an everlasting love, shining in the same effulgence and bathed in the same ineffable love of the Son for the Mother and the Mother for the Son, Mary will be enthroned beside Jesus and will share with the Divine Lamb the praises and the love of the Blessed. So true it is that to love Jesus is necessarily to love his Mother."

Venerable Anthony Kowalczyk (1866–1947)

It warms my heart to remember Brother Anthony Kowalczyk, as I had the privilege of meeting him several times before his death in 1947. I have vivid recollections of walking in the front door of St. John's College in Edmonton and seeing him sweeping the corridors. He would stop and come over to greet me warmly, kissing my hand to show his great respect for priests. I would slip him a dollar to help him build a grotto to Our Lady in the yard. Towards the end of his life this project was the joy of his heart.

Born in Poland on June 4, 1866, Brother Anthony was the sixth of twelve children in a close-knit peasant family that lived in the village of Dziersanow, near the Shrine of Lutogniew, with its miraculous picture of Our Lady, Comforter of the Afflicted.

Following his apprenticeship as a blacksmith, his family's tight finances forced him to emigrate to Germany and become a factory-worker in Hamburg and Cologne. Beginning to go blind from the searing heat of the furnace in the steel foundry where he worked, he was given back his sight unimpaired while making the Stations of the Cross at a nearby church.

In 1891 he entered the novitiate of the Oblates of Mary Immaculate in Holland. A year later he pronounced his temporary vows as a brother in the order, hoping to be posted to the foreign missions. At last, in May 1896, he was sent across the Atlantic to the important Oblate Mission of Lac La Biche, a supply station some 175 miles northeast of Edmonton, to be the engineer for the grist and saw mills there.

At Lac La Biche, on July 15, 1897, Brother Anthony crushed his right hand while sawing lumber. To save his life, the limb had to be amputated without anesthetic. After his recovery, in October of the same year, he and his machinery were sent to St. Paul des Metis, a colony that was part of a great effort of evangelization by the Oblate missionaries among the Metis. Eventually, in 1909, it had to be abandoned and St. Paul des Metis became known simply as St. Paul.

There Brother Anthony worked endless hours to help keep the colony going and alleviate the poverty and suffering of the Metis. Over and above his other chores, he even grew a vegetable garden for them and did any blacksmithing they needed done. For four years he and the other brothers lived in a converted pig sty. Eventually he asked his superior to lighten a workload that had become overwhelming. The rigid superior took this amiss and forbade Brother Anthony to receive the Eucharist on weekdays for three months. Brother Anthony was so wounded by this penance that one day he burst into sobs. Although he submitted without complaint, it must have taxed his humility greatly, for he was by nature a quick-tempered man.

In 1911 he was transferred to St. John's College, a boarding school for boys run by the Oblates in Edmonton, where he laboured until his death. Despite the loss of his right hand, he served as the college maintenance man, janitor, blacksmith, furnace stoker, laundryman, bell ringer and sacristan. He also tended its large garden and was caretaker of its chickens, pigs and horses.

Brother Anthony was a great friend to the students. He fixed their hockey sticks, sharpened their skates, repaired their watches and mended the frames of their eyeglasses. He went out of his way to comfort new students who had left home for the first time and were lonely, his favorite prescription for homesickness being, "Say a Hail Mary."

Although a simple man of few, halting words, he showed such deep and humble faith that he had a great influence in the college. With the passing of the years his reputation as a living saint grew. Many people came to him asking for small miracles, and he obliged. Once, for example, a boy lost his return ticket to Winnipeg and asked Brother Anthony for help. The Brother immediately dropped to his knees in prayer. Then he went out the door and minutes later returned with the ticket in his hand, having found it in the snow.

In the 1940's his superiors decided that a grotto of Our Lady of Lourdes should be erected on the college grounds. It was left to him to gather the stones and beg the funds for it, inasmuch as all his life he had had a deep devotion to his "Good Mother" and had prayed the Rosary, her "Gospel of the Poor". After the grotto was built, he used to spend a long time there in prayer almost every evening until his death on July 10, 1947.

A friend of mine, Father Paul-Émile Breton, O.M.I., who wrote *Blacksmith of God*, the first biography of Brother Anthony, writes in his introduction:

"I wanted above all to point out the strength of his soul. This humble lay Brother was far from developing a sentimental devotion. He had a harsh spiritual existence, which we may compare to that of a blacksmith. He fought and he suffered. His soul was forged by sacrifices, ordeals and self-denials."

I remember well when his cause for beatification was opened in 1952. The Oblate vice-postulator came to see me and invited me to assist him in the process. To my everlasting regret, I was unable to accept this unique privilege at the time. Devotion to Brother Anthony has grown rapidly. The authorities receive letters from all over the world which relate the favours obtained through his intercession. His name has become synonymous with peace, joy, and humble good humour. One day, for instance, one of the Oblate priests, who had asked him for prayers for the healing of his youngest sister, teased him, imitating his limping English: "Blessed Virgin no good; me ask you to pray for my sister; nothing happens." "No, no," Brother Anthony replied, unfazed, "Blessed Virgin good; my prayers no good."

Several biographical accounts have been written about Brother Anthony, and videotapes have been made on his life. Schools and convents bear his name. People pray to him for favours, and many visit his grave at the Oblate Cemetery in St. Albert. Here at Madonna House, our men have a special devotion to him, taking courage from the heroic example of his silent eloquence.

In 1969 Cardinal Karol Wojtyla, the future Pope John Paul II, visited his grave. We pray that, by the grace of God, he may be the Pope to beatify him.

Pauline Landry (1930–1951)

Pauline Landry was born three months premature on June 22, 1930, so tiny that her head could fit into a cup. Her mother, Éliane, a nurse, wrapped the baby girl in swaddling-clothes and laid her on the oven door, using it as a crude incubator. At the same time, she entrusted her frail, little daughter to the care of Our Lady of the Cape, since the day of her birth was the anniversary of the miracle there. Later in her short life, Pauline was to say, "God loved me first and Mary loved me from the first day of my life." When, in August, little Pauline cried for the first time, the whole family rejoiced.

Pauline was raised on a farm at St. Sulpice, a few miles from Montreal, on the banks of the St. Lawrence River. She was her mother's second child, but her father's 15th, for he had been married three times. When she was four, she began to experience the first symptoms of her lifelong intestinal illness. The next year she had an operation for appendicitis, from which she never really recovered fully. At age nine she needed still more surgery to remove an intestinal tumour.

Despite her on-going health problems, Pauline proved to be a first-class student. After her primary schooling she and her sister, Marcelle, were sent to the well-known boarding school run by the Sisters of Saint Anne in Rawdon.

Desiring to become a teacher, Pauline attended the normal school at Valleyfield, where she stayed with her mother's sister and her family. For the next three years, she was happy in these surroundings, excelling in her studies despite her declining health. Finally she became so weak that she was forced to quit the normal school. With her bright, active intelligence Pauline found this a heartbreaking outcome to all her hard work. Her teachers, the Sisters of the Holy Names of Jesus and Mary, advised her to do volunteer work at the Marian Service of Montreal.

At the age of 18, Pauline came knocking at the door of the Marian Service, humbly offering to do "any little trifling jobs". The other members of this apostolate discovered her gifts of mind and heart, and, for three years, until her death, she became a key member of their team, helping them with the publication and distribution of their little journal, *The Marian Digest*. Pauline read St. Louis de Montfort's *True Devotion* and made her consecration to Jesus through Mary on the feast of the Visitation. After that, she turned to Our Lady for everything with utter confidence, not only for the strength she needed to cope with her chronically poor health, but for the grace to overcome her exaggerated fear of displeasing the Lord. Beset by these physical and moral trials, Pauline found happiness in her work for Our Lady, caught up, like St. Louis de Montfort, in the joyful expectation that a Marian era would precede the return of Christ. The last three years of her life were totally dedicated to Jesus through Mary.

Whenever her illness forced her to spend time in bed, she would use the time to pray and offer herself to Our Lady. She had a particular love for the Miraculous Medal, which she wore around her neck, calling it "my only jewel".

One evening, two or three weeks before Pauline's death, while she and her mother were reciting the Rosary, her mother saw a light illumine the crucifix before them. She said nothing, but at the end of the Rosary, when she got up, she noticed that Pauline, still on her knees, was radiant. A few minutes later, Pauline got ready to go to bed in her room, where she usually kept a night-light on the table. Embracing her mother, she exclaimed, "Mom, you can put out my night light. I don't need it, now that Mary has given me a better one." Our Lady had visited her, in keeping with the words of *Revelation*:

"His servants shall worship him; they shall see his face, and his name shall be on their foreheads. And night shall be no more; they need no light of lamp or sun, for the Lord God will be their light, and they shall reign for ever and ever" (Rev 22: 3-5).

From then until her death she was radiantly joyful, her pale, wasted face transfigured by an inner light: "I am happy," she explained, "I don't have any more fears. Now I am enveloped by the mantle of Mama Mary."

Pauline worked for the Marian Service until two days before she died, even though she was thin and weak, wracked by illness. On November 15, 1951 she stayed in bed. Her brother Bernard, a priest, gave her the Sacrament of the Sick and read her the consecration prayer of St. Louis de Montfort. The next day, at 4:30 p.m., she entered the Father's house, 21 years old.

By chance, the funeral director offered Pauline's father a blue coffin for her remains. While Marie-Thérèse Chevalier, the friend and co-worker whom she called her "spiritual mother", was praying at Pauline's coffin, she felt a surge of faith and joy. "I knew," she recounts, "that my little girl was experiencing the joy of paradise in the presence of Our Lord and Our Lady. Why should I weep when she was so happy?"

After her funeral people began praying to her and obtaining favours. A letter which she had addressed to Marie-Thérèse was found after her death: "Little Mother, you may think that I have left you. Here on earth I always tried to obey you. In Heaven, I will support you in whatever way Mama Mary lets me; I will try to do everything that you want."

Shortly before Pauline's passing, the Marian Service had published a pamphlet to celebrate the first anniversary of the local Rosary Crusade, which left them a debt of $6,500. When they began praying to Pauline, the money came, as if miraculously from heaven, allowing them to pay the printer in full! Pauline herself had once remarked, "How can we worry about paying off our material debts? If our good mother is powerful enough to save us from the demons' tentacles, she can just as easily settle all our financial difficulties. All we need is faith and more faith."

On the Feast of the Assumption of Our Lady in 1953, a special celebration was held at Pauline's original home parish of St. Sulpice. Cardinal Paul-Émile Léger, the Archbishop of Montreal, was on hand to bless a magnificent statue of Mary, Mediatrix of All Graces. Thousands of people had come from several dioceses to honour their Mother and one of her beloved daughters, Pauline Landry.

Georges Vanier (1888-1967) Governor General of Canada

The eldest of five children, Georges Vanier was born in Montreal on April 23, 1888 to a French-Canadian father and an Irish mother. An earnest, considerate boy, he was sent to Loyola College, run by the Jesuits, at the age of nine. In 1906, when he graduated, he was the prefect of the Sodality of Our Lady at the school. From there, perfectly bilingual, he went on to study law at Laval University and was admitted to the bar at 23.

At the outset of World War I, he began a period of distinguished military service with the 22nd French-Canadian Battalion or "Van Doos", winning many medals for bravery. Just weeks before the signing of the Armistice in 1918 he lost his right leg in battle.

In 1921 he married Pauline Archer, with whom he had five children, one of them being the celebrated Jean Vanier, founder of the L'Arche Communities. After the War he went on to have a distinguished career with the League of Nations and the Canadian Diplomatic Service, as well as the Army.

During World War II, Vanier worked as Canada's representative with General de Gaulle. Afterwards, in 1946, he was appointed Canadian Ambassador to Paris, where he met Cardinal Angelo Roncalli, who later became Pope John XXIII. The two became lifelong friends. His notes from this period show a deepening prayer life, fed by his daily attendance at Mass and meditation, as well as extensive spiritual reading. In an entry for the Feast of the Assumption, 1952, he remarks that his life underwent a dramatic change that day: "Mary's day of glory marked a turning point in my spiritual life." A year later, on the Feast of Pentecost in 1953, he experienced yet another milestone in his spiritual development. While praying after Mass he was given a vivid, mystical sense that he enjoyed a personal relationship with Our Lady and the Blessed Trinity.

Vanier was called out of retirement to become Governor General of Canada from 1959 until his death on March 5, 1967. One of his first decisions was to establish a private chapel in the Governor General's residence in Ottawa. The Vaniers attended daily Mass there, and he and his wife took turns visiting the Blessed Sacrament throughout the day. General Vanier became well known for his habit of not making any important decision without first consulting Christ in the Eucharist. When Canadian Prime Minister John Diefenbaker phoned to ask his advice about some of the problems he had running the country, at the end of the conversation he would add, "I do not ask an immediate answer. I know that there is Someone else you have to consult."

When Queen Elizabeth visited Ottawa in 1964 and was received in the Governor General's residence, Vanier showed her the house and gently brought her to the chapel, putting her at ease by saying, "Do not think that you are obliged to come to this chapel." As it happened, the Queen did take the opportunity to pray there frequently during her stay, even attending Mass one day. Later she said of her host, "I understand where he gets his wisdom, his strength, his serenity. I felt God very especially present in that little chapel."

The Vaniers' chapel was dedicated to Our Lady of the Immaculate Conception and was officially opened on her feastday, the 8th of December. The chapel reflected the two great objects of General Vanier's devotion: the Eucharist and Our Lady. For him the two went hand in hand.

Georges Vanier went frequently to Lourdes and recognized that the many spiritual miracles that were being performed there were far greater than the physical ones. "Hundreds of thousands of people come each year without being physically cured," he remarked, "but all leave Lourdes full of peace and serenity, not in the least disappointed."

General Vanier's official coat of arms was emblazoned with a Latin phrase from the "Our Father": *Fiat voluntas tua*, "Thy will be done." Along the upper half of this coat of arms, in honour of Our Lady, is a small holm-oak, representing the tree above which she appeared to the children at Fatima. General Vanier even wrote a prayer to Our Lady for Canada.

When he died, the whole nation lamented his passing. Everyone testified to his Christian greatness, feeling that they had lost a genuine friend. Since then schools have been built in his honour, and even a city has been named after him. As well, the cause for his beatification been opened.

At the time of his death, Catherine Doherty wrote:

"It was by his love of all of us, which somehow escaped in utter simplicity and approachability, that he was able to bring God closer to us... ." (*Restoration*, April 1967, Volume XX).

No doubt even now, from heaven, he is still bringing God closer to us.

Pauline Vanier (1898–1991)

An only child, Pauline Vanier was born into a distinguished Montreal family on March 18, 1898. Her father, Charles Archer, the chief justice of the Superior Court of Quebec, was of English ancestry, while her mother, Thérèse, was descended from the prominent seigneurial family of de Salaberry, which had first come to Canada in 1730. From age eight to twelve she was sent to the Sacred Heart Convent in Montreal for her schooling. The rest of her education she received at home under governesses and tutors. Her spiritual development, however, came under the strong influence of her mother, who put her faith into practice, taking Pauline with her on visits to the poor.

"My spiritual life in my childhood was very open and wonderful, due to my mother," Pauline has written. "She had been formed in a spirituality which was totally opposed to the Jansenistic atmosphere of the times. Her spiritual director had been Father Pichon, a French religious, who had been, before his coming to Canada, the confessor of St. Thérèse of the Child Jesus in the Carmel of Lisieux. This is to say that my mother had a spiritual life based upon growth and development in love, and I, at the age of six, made my First Communion, sitting on Father Pichon's knees. He was my mother's spiritual director for 36 years and, of course, his direction radiated into my life."

In the wake of World War I, she married Georges Vanier. Together they matured spiritually, reinforcing each another and their children. It was by the good graces of his wife that Georges shed some of his tendencies to a stern, Jansenistic faith, in order to embrace a God whose main characteristic is a fathomless love for his creatures. The couple's spiritual life came to be very much influenced by the way of the Carmelites, with their strong focus on Our Lady, who leads all believers to her Son. All through her husband's career, Madame Vanier took a special interest in the poor and less fortunate.

Pauline's life was not without its trials and tribulations. During the 1930's she lapsed into a state of chronic depression: "It was a bad period and I'm ashamed to say it went on for almost seven years." At another time she went through a dark night of the soul for about two years. Her Trappist son, Father Benedict, reminded her of the Gospel passage in which Christ slept during a storm, while his disciples fretted. "Yes," she said, "I understand. The Lord sleeps, but he is there. In moments like these, what a gift is faith."

Madame Vanier loved to mention the friends who had helped her to develop a strong faith: Father René Voillaune, founder of the Little Brothers of Jesus; Pope John XXIII, a personal friend; Brother Roger Schutz, founder of Taizé; Jacques and Raissa Maritain; and the Carmelites. There were other, less well-known influences. She was struck, for example, by a cleaning lady she met in the subway, who was on her way to a Communist meeting to testify to Christ.

Madame Vanier had a strong mothering instinct, which manifested itself in her loving concern for people right across the social spectrum, especially the poor. One day she invited Catherine Doherty to tea at Rideau Hall, the Governor General's residence. When they met, they recognized each other immediately as soul sisters.

On March 5, 1967, her husband of nearly 50 years passed over to the Father. Retiring to Montreal after her husband's death, she went through a period of spiritual restlessness and anguished soul-searching. Gradually she realized that Madame had to be replaced by "Mamie", as she came to be called in the last part of her life.

The transformation happened in this way. In 1964, her son, Jean, had founded an organization called L'Arche ("The Ark") to take care of mentally handicapped. At first, both his father and mother were doubtful about the project, but the enthusiasm with which it was received all over the world quickly changed their minds. Five years after her husband's death, at the age of 74, Pauline left for the headquarters of L'Arche in Trosly-Breuil, northeast of Paris, to become the mama of everyone there, the volunteers as well as the handicapped.

Her spiritual equilibrium was much tested for the next 18 years, for the move to L'Arche required a further, radical stripping of self, forcing her to greater depths of conversion. Mamie began to be reshaped by the Mother of God, who is the mother of us all. By the grace of God, with much prayer, she gradually began to receive with great tenderness and unconditional love "all the little lame ducks," to whom she became a serene and consoling grandmother. Her favorite prayer in those years was "Mary, take me by the hand and lead me to the heart of Jesus."

Mamie passed over to the arms of Our Lady on March 23, 1991, in France. Her funeral was held in the Notre Dame Basilica of Quebec City, and she was buried next to her husband in the Citadel of Quebec, where they had experienced so many happy moments. Madame Vanier was queenly in her bearing and intelligence and in the greatness of her heart. Nonetheless she will be remembered not so much for these immensely attractive qualities as for her humility, simplicity, and openness to every person she met, for Mamie was one who had modelled her life on that of the Blessed Virgin Mary.

Annette Desautels (1924–1982)
Victim Soul for Priests

Bed-ridden for the last 30 years of her life, Annette Desautels suffered from multiple sclerosis. Unable even to sit in a wheelchair, she had to be carried by stretcher wherever she went. Witnesses have described the extraordinary love and joy that radiated from her in the midst of her infirmities.

Born in Montreal on December 10, 1924, Annette was the eldest in a family of four boys and two girls. Her early schooling was with the Sisters of St. Anne at St. Arsène School, from which she went on to Ange Gardien, a boarding school in St. Henri. As a young girl, she joined the Children of Mary and was active with the Young Catholic Students.

On her twentieth birthday she became a Third Order Dominican, choosing St. Catherine of Siena as her patron. Years later, in 1980, when the Third Order Dominicans celebrated their centenary, Annette was chosen as their woman of the year, being described as "the mystic and contemplative rose that adorns our confraternity of Our Lady of the Rosary".

As she came to be afflicted with serious health problems, she made a conscious decision that she would unite her sufferings with those of Christ for the salvation of priests. In 1947 she entered the novitiate of the Little Sisters of the Assumption, but was heartbroken when she had to leave the order in 1951 on account of her failing health. For a while she felt a little stronger and tried working as a nurse's aide in a sanatorium. Soon she experienced more and more symptoms of her illness. Stepping down from the curbs of sidewalks, for instance, became a dangerous ordeal. Still, wanting to help her family with their finances, every morning she set off courageously to work. Often she had to return home before the end of her workday or before her day was even begun. Diagnosed as having multiple sclerosis, she entered the Convalescent Hospital in Montreal, staying there until 1955.

In 1955, still able to write with her own hand, she sent this note to her friend Rita:

"Together let us allow Mary to give us to Jesus. This is the surest, most wonderful way of dying, truly in Love and for

Love. May each day, each hour, each occasion, be a moment in which Mama may help us to die to self and to every creature, so as to live in him, lose ourselves in him, in his Divine Heart... The more a child is small and weak, the more its mother takes care of it. Therefore, I am sure Mary will take good care of both of us."

When Annette's condition deteriorated still further, she was forced to find a new place to live. On February 16, 1955, after a novena to Our Lady of Lourdes, Annette was received as a permanent guest at the Foyer de Charité (i.e. The Hostel of Love), founded by Cardinal Léger in 1951, at Pointe-aux-Trembles, Montreal. There, each day, she was brought on a stretcher to Mass. In the afternoon she would make a visit to the Blessed Sacrament and stay for the recitation of the Rosary.

A week after her arrival she wrote again to Rita: "You must rejoice and truly be convinced that I am fully happy and cherished here at the Foyer, grateful to heaven and full of hope... everything is a gift from Our Lady, the Immaculate." God favoured her with an intimate sense of union with Our Lady. On her sickbed she would sing Marian hymns and say the Rosary, even though her palsied fingers could not hold the beads. As St. Louis de Montfort urges, she had thrown herself into Mary as a stone is thrown into the deepest sea. She described the phenomenon to Rita: "The more I throw myself into her, the more perhaps, I will be able to lose myself, and not finding myself anymore, I shall discover him."

Despite her physical limitations and her severely curtailed mobility, she was able to undertake a vast apostolate of suffering whose true extent and influence no one knows, except God. Annette's hospitality never faltered, no matter how ill she felt. She received each person as Christ, praying: "Lord, make of me a proclaimer of the Gospel, one who communicates to others the convictions of her faith. A proclaimer of the Gospel, full of peace and serene optimism. A proclaimer of the Gospel who announces to all, by her life and her witness, that you are there, present to our world and in each person."

Annette was a great listener who prayed fervently for anyone who confided in her. She had many sleepless nights, totally given over to prayer, meditation and reflection. Unable to use her hands, she dictated her reflections. With the help of devoted secretaries, she managed to produce three books. Several times television cameras recorded her life and sayings. On a number of occasions she was transported from the Foyer on a stretcher to give her witness story as a Christian invalid.

In her last years, her spiritual director, Father Ovila Bélanger, asked her to write out some of her reflections on Our Lady. Annette replied, "I won't have time. I will die soon." All the same, he urged her: "Write. Write whatever comes." Thus she commented on the *Angelus* and the *Salve Regina*, for example.

In 1982, on July 11, 12 and 13, Annette seemed to have been drawn into another world, living in an ecstatic state, as if she was already experiencing the beatific vision. On July 13, she exclaimed to Claire, her secretary: "I want to shout to the whole world that the Gospel is true. For so many (who are) suffering, he has deigned to use the little instrument that I am, to bring a little peace. He is good... What is being prepared will be immensely beautiful, because Jesus is coming to heal our great wounds, all the wounds of the hearts of men. How I bless him for everything he has deigned to bring in the way of joy, peace, and suffering."

On the 26th of that same month, Cardinal Paul-Émile Léger celebrated Mass at the Foyer and visited Annette, who whispered to him, "I am praying much for you." The next day, friends and relatives surrounded her bed for most of the day. At one point they sang the *Salve Regina*, and her face became luminous.

At 9:10 a.m., on July 28, the Lord came to gather to himself the one who had lived so totally for him in the company of Mary. Two days later, the Cardinal himself presided at Annette's funeral Mass, surrounded by 15 concelebrants, with the chapel filled to overflowing. Because she died on my 65th birthday, I feel a special closeness to her.

Catherine de Hueck Doherty (1896–1985) Foundress, Madonna House Lay Apostolate

The founding genius of Madonna House was born in Russia on August 15, 1896 into an ancient culture that was thoroughly steeped in Christianity. Her parents, Theodore and Emma Kolyschkine, who belonged to the minor nobility, were devout members of the Orthodox Church and had their child baptized in St. Petersburg on September 15 (New Style calendar), the day that is now observed as the feast of Our Lady of Sorrows. Two aspects of her upbringing that she carried with her for the rest of her long and eventful life were a love for the poor and a tender devotion to the Mother of God. "I remember as a little girl," she relates, "gathering wild flowers on a hill and putting them at the feet of the Virgin in a Russian shrine."

Schooled abroad because of her father's job, she and her family returned to St. Petersburg in 1910, where she was enrolled in the prestigious Princess Obolensky Academy. In 1912, aged 15, she made what turned out to be a disastrous marriage with her first cousin, Boris de Hueck.

At the outbreak of World War I, Catherine became a Red Cross nurse at the front, experiencing the horrors of battle firsthand. On her return to St. Petersburg, she and Boris barely escaped the turmoil of the Russian Revolution with their lives, nearly starving to death as refugees in Finland. Together they made their way to England, where Catherine was received into the Catholic Church on November 27, 1919.

Emigrating to Canada with Boris, Catherine gave birth to their only child, George, in Toronto in 1921. Soon she and Boris became more and more painfully estranged from one another, as he pursued his extramarital affairs. To make ends meet, Catherine took various jobs and eventually became a lecturer, travelling a circuit that took her across North America.

Prosperous now, but deeply dissatisfied with a life of material comfort, her marriage in ruins, she began to feel the promptings of a deeper call through a passage that leaped to her eyes every time she opened the Scriptures: "Arise, go... sell all you possess... take up your cross and follow me." Consulting with various priests and the bishop of the diocese, she began her lay apostolate among the poor in Toronto in the early 1930's, calling it Friendship House. She desired to become simple, poor, and trusting in God like a child.

Because her approach was so different from what was being done at the time, she encountered much persecution and resistance, especially at the hands of the clergy. One significant exception was Archbishop Neil McNeil of Toronto, who proved to be a staunch friend and supporter. Notwithstanding, Friendship House was forced to close in 1936. Catherine then went to Europe and spent a year investigating Catholic Action. On her return, she was given the chance to revive Friendship House in New York City among the poor in Harlem. After that she was invited to open another Friendship House in Chicago.

In 1943, having received an annulment of her first marriage, she married Eddie Doherty, one of America's foremost reporters, who had fallen in love with her while writing a story about her apostolate. That summer they took a vacation in Combermere, Ontario and felt drawn to the area, buying a house there.

Meanwhile, serious disagreements had arisen between the staff of Friendship House and its foundress. When these could not be resolved, Catherine and Eddie moved permanently to Combermere on May 17, 1947, naming their new rural apostolate Madonna House in honour of Our Lady. Although it seemed like the end of all her dreams at the time, this was to be the seedbed of an apostolate that now numbers more than 200 staff workers and over 125 associate priests, deacons, and bishops, with 22 field-houses throughout the world.

A critical event in the history and growth of Madonna House occurred on February 2, 1951, when Catherine and Eddie dedicated their lives to Jesus through Mary, using the consecration of St. Louis de Montfort. In a new way, Madonna House fell under the protective mantle of the Mother of God, whom Catherine had begun to invoke as Our Lady of Combermere. It was due to this consecration, Catherine believed, that eventually the Madonna House Apostolate would be given permanent status in the Church as an association of celibate men, women, and priests, living together in community and devoting themselves to the poor. Nurtured by her devotion to the Mother of God, Catherine's spiritual life came to full flower in the 1950's, as she began to integrate her rich Eastern heritage with that of the Western Church, laying the groundwork for modern classics like *Poustinia*. Also, to be like the other staff workers, she and Eddie agreed to live the rest of their lives in celibate chastity, even though they were a married couple. The chapel at Madonna House was consecrated to the Immaculate Conception by Father John Callahan, the first director general of priests, on December 8, 1953. On June 8, 1960 the life-size bronze statue of Our Lady of Combermere was blessed by Bishop Smith of Pembroke, marking a further Marian milestone in the development of Madonna House.

Catherine stresses time and again throughout her writings that Mary is the gateway to Jesus: "If you don't know her, you will never fully know her Son." In a later book on Our Lady, entitled *Bogoroditza* (Russian word meaning "She Who Gave Birth to God" or "Mother of God"), she explains the deeper wellsprings of her devotion:

"We Russians have no 'special devotion' to Our Lady because she's just as much a part and parcel of our life as breathing. It's impossible to have devotion to breathing! I don't have any devotion to taking air in and letting it out—it's my life. If I stop breathing, I die. That's the way it is."*

By the time Catherine Doherty died on December 14, 1985 in Combermere at the age of 89, Our Lady had firmly established the apostolate named after her. Since then, the cause for Catherine's beatification has been officially opened.

Cardinal Paul-Émile Léger (1904–1991)

I first heard of Paul-Émile Léger in the fall of 1940. His cousin, Monsignor Maxime Pilon, my first pastor in Morinville, Alberta, told me how his cousin was fast becoming famous in the Province of Quebec as an eloquent preacher.

Cardinal Léger's extraordinary career took its rise in the quiet village of St. Anicet, near Valleyfield, Quebec, close to the American border, where he was born on April 25, 1904, one of two children. His parents owned the general store and were so busy running it that he spent much time with his maternal grandmother: "She gave me tenderness and introduced me to the real faith of my religion."

Even as a boy attending the parish schoolhouse in St. Anicet, he showed high intelligence and love of learning, coupled with an exceptional flair for public speaking. Recognizing

---

* *Bogoroditza* (Combermere, ON: Madonna House Publications, 1999) p. 125.

his gifts, his parents decided to send him to the Minor Seminary of Sainte Thérèse for a classical education. In September, 1925, Léger entered the Grand Seminary in Montreal and was ordained a priest on May 25, 1929. Then he joined the Sulpicians, a teaching order, making his novitiate at Issy-les-Moulineaux in France, where he was stationed afterwards as a seminary professor.

In 1932 his superiors asked him to go to Japan to help establish a seminary. Summoned back to Quebec in 1939, he was appointed the vicar-general of his home diocese of Valleyfield, spending seven busy years there. During this time he began to establish his reputation as a superb preacher, with a brilliant command of the French language. His next posting, beginning in the autumn of 1947, was as the rector of the Canadian Pontifical College in Rome, where he made a deep impression on Pope Pius XII, who named him as the Archbishop of Montreal on March 19, 1950. Before returning home to Montreal, he sent this message by cable to his flock: "The little ones, the humble, the poor, the sick, and the workers will be the chosen portion of our fold." He soon showed he meant what he had said by establishing the Foyer de Charité or "Hostel of Love", a refuge for the poor and neglected.

Three years later, in 1953, he was elected to the College of Cardinals. During his very first years as chief shepherd of the Catholics of Montreal, he launched a campaign to promote the family Rosary, becoming known as "the Rosary bishop". Each night the Rosary was broadcast from his chapel to people all across the province on radio station CKAC.

Cardinal Léger was indeed a Marian Bishop. "Let us seek our Marian inspiration in the authentic doctrine of the Church," he said in 1955, speaking to a group of educators gathered together under the auspices of the city's Marian Service. "Let us try to become disciples of Mary in following, for example, that father of Marian doctrine, St. Louis de

Montfort. I congratulate the Marian Service of the diocese for organizing these days for educators on this feast of the Queenship of Mary. This Marian Service works in hidden ways, but accomplishes great things. It upholds public opinion. It spreads its influence everywhere, bringing the Marian message over the radio waves every day, so that Mary can enter every family and every home. It works to place the Virgin Mary where she belongs — at the very heart of our life and our activities. The Marian Service is an apostolic service. There are always two aspects in the activity of the Church: prayer and action. These two forms must be united in such a way as not to break the harmony of the Mystical Body. Action must be an expression that overflows from contemplation. Apostolic action takes its source in meditation. After Pentecost, the Apostles entered resolutely into action. They gave their lives as witnesses to the mission that had been entrusted to them. The Blessed Virgin encouraged and advised them. She was their star and their sure support. She was and remains the Queen of Apostles. She is responsible for the whole heart. She shines on our actions like the sun, which is the source of germination upon earth. She will always remain above action. She must give action its apostolic fecundity.

"The Holy Spirit does not entrust her with such a particular mission. She is above missions, for apostolic missions will transform the earth in the measure in which the Blessed Virgin will flood them with her grace. ...May this vision of the universal apostolate in Mary be for us... a source of confidence, for if we place ourselves under her protection, depending upon her, we shall accomplish marvels of grace and our work will be most efficacious."

By the time of Vatican II, in 1962, Cardinal Léger had acquired a widespread reputation as a joyful man of God and faithful servant of the Church. At the Council, drawing on his wisdom as a pastor and teacher, he exercised a calming, beneficial influence, as he tried to bridge the gap between the various factions.

In 1967, after 17 years as pastor of the see of Montreal, he made a momentous announcement. Mentioning that he had given thousands of speeches over the years, he continued by saying, "Now I must pass from speech to action", and then announced his decision to resign and become a simple missionary, working among the lepers in Cameroon. His example of loving service to the poorest of the poor was earthshaking news at the time, especially in the Catholic world.

After several years in Africa, he returned to Montreal in 1979, where he lived in semi-retirement until his death in 1991, continuing his work for the poor by helping his brother, Jules, who was Governor General of Canada, to establish a charitable foundation.

The Jules and Paul-Émile Léger Foundation co-ordinates and supports many educational, religious, and philanthropic activities in Canada and elsewhere. In death no less than in life, therefore, Cardinal Léger's legacy of charity endures, for he was a true son and disciple of the Blessed Virgin Mary, the Mother of God.

Monsignor Ralph J. Egan (1901–1997)

In the late 1950's, when I was already a member of Madonna House, I made a pilgrimage to the Shrine of the Canadian Martyrs in Midland, Ontario. On the way back, as has been my practice all through my life as a priest, I paid a visit to the local pastor. Now Madonna House at that time was often regarded with suspicion as a strange new phenomenon, somewhat dubious in the way it grouped together laymen, laywomen, and priests. So, as I rang the doorbell, I was ready for anything. It would not have surprised me much, when I said, "I'm Father Brière from Madonna House", if the priest had slammed the door in my face. But not at all. Opening the door wide, he welcomed me, "Come right in," and we had a wonderful visit. His name was Monsignor Ralph J. Egan, a holy, humble man.

We soon became good friends and I agreed to be his spiritual director. I can witness, from an intimate knowledge of his soul, to his virtues and the devotion he had to Our Lady and Jesus in the Blessed Eucharist. He cherished his priesthood and the Mass, which he said with deep reverence. I knew all the things he struggled with, all his worries and concerns, and can testify to the holiness of his life, founded on faith, hope, and love.

Born in Toronto on January 10, 1901, Monsignor Egan was ordained on June 11, 1927 and died February 8, 1997, having spent nearly 70 years as a diocesan priest. Early in his life he had been a newspaper man and remained one at heart, convinced of the power of the printed word in whatever form. At one time, he himself published a little newspaper on the Legion of Mary which was distributed free of charge.

When Monsignor Egan saw the hunger for love felt by many of God's people, he thought that the best antidote to loneliness, poverty, depression and the forces of evil is the power of good, broadcast and disseminated as far and wide as possible. What came to his mind were the words of St. Maximilian Kolbe: "The earth needs to be flooded by a mighty deluge of Catholic and Marian literature, written in every language and reaching every country, so as to drown in the waves of truth all those voices of error that have been using the printing press as their most powerful ally. The globe must be encircled by the words of life in printed form, so that the world may once again experience the joy of living."

In his later years, stimulated by these words, Monsignor Egan envisioned Our Lady's message being received by her children in many places by means of the printed word. He saw thousands of pieces of literature flooding all the towns and cities of Canada. His vision began to be realized in 1990 when, close to 90, he founded the St. Maximilian Kolbe Apostolate of the Printed Word. With two lay people and a De La Salle Brother, Monsignor Egan set out to distribute, free of charge, Catholic printed materials to the parishes in Toronto. Beginning with only the meager supply of items that Monsignor Egan had accumulated through the years, the four apostles started handing out pamphlets, rosaries, holy cards, and Legion of Mary tesserae. What little they had started out with multiplied rapidly thanks to donations from publishers and other groups.

Today St. Maximilian Kolbe Apostolate for the Printed Word operates an office in the basement of St. Peter's Church in Toronto, with two administrative staff looking after the requests from individuals, schools, and parishes for Catholic booklets, prayer cards and other religious materials. This apostolate aims to spread the Word to the world through the printed word. As St. Anthony Mary Claret said, "Since we cannot send missionaries everywhere, let us send good books which can do as much as the missionaries themselves."

The apostolate has grown remarkably, holding monthly Eucharistic adorations, fostering Rosary devotion at schools, promoting the Legion of Mary, and distributing literature to all who request it, including prisons and overseas missions.

More Canadians Who Loved Our Lady

Among other Canadians who had a great love for Our Lady, special mention may be made of the following:

Rosalie Cadron-Jetté, 1794-1864. Foundress of the Sisters of Mercy. Her congregation was established in Montreal in 1850 to house and care for single mothers. She is recognized as an icon of the tenderness of Jesus and his Mother.

Father Onésime Brousseau, 1853-1920. Founder of the Congregation of the Sisters of Our Lady of Perpetual Help and of the Brothers of Our Lady of the Fields.

Father Alexis-Louis Mangin, 1857-1920. Founder of the Servants of Jesus-Mary, who wrote: "Consider what perfection can be contained in the little heart of a Servant of Jesus-Mary. This great perfection is the work of the Holy Spirit through Mary... ."

Marie de la Rousselière, 1840-1924. She founded the shrine of Our Lady of Reparation in Montreal. She had published, at her own expense, an edition of St. Louis de Montfort's *True Devotion to Mary*. Afterwards, this book became a principal tool used in spreading devotion to Mary throughout Canada.

Father Elzéar Delamarre, 1854-1925. As rector of the Seminary of Chicoutimi, he founded a religious congregation, The Antonian Sisters of Mary, to be at the service of Christ the priest. At Lake Bouchette he established a shrine dedicated to Our Lady of Lourdes.

Alexandre Charette, 1861-1932, Montreal. A master plumber and a fervent member of the Sodality of Mary from the age of 21 until his death. His love for Our Lady led him to a love of Jesus in the Blessed Sacrament, prompting him to take part in nocturnal adoration at Notre Dame. He devoted himself to the care of orphans and abandoned women, establishing a soup kitchen and a home for the homeless through the Conference of St. Vincent de Paul. He was also the grandfather of Marie-Thérèse Chevalier, who has dedicated her whole life to the Marian apostolate since 1948.

Bishop Ovide Charlebois, O.M.I., 1862-1933. Heroic Marian Bishop of the Keewatin.

Father Alexandre-Albert Godbout, 1879-1949. An outstanding apostle of Our Lady in the Archdiocese of Quebec. At St. Francis of Assisi parish in Quebec, he established a shrine to Our Lady of Roc Amadour at the spot where, in 1536, Jacques Cartier led the first pilgrimage to Our Lady in New France.

Jeanne Dépatie, 1910-1955. For several years she spent entire nights reciting the Rosary in the chapel of Our Lady of Lourdes in Montreal.

Father Victor Lelièvre, 1876-1956. A celebrated Oblate of Mary Immaculate who dedicated his life to spreading devotion to the Sacred Heart and the Blessed Virgin Mary, especially among the working class.

Emma Curotte, 1890-1961. Foundress of the Shrine of Our Lady Queen of All Hearts in Chertsey in the Diocese of Joliette in 1943.

Father Henri Roy, O.M.I., 1898-1965. Founder of the Young Christian Workers in Canada. Founder, as well, of the Secular Institute of Pius X, he placed it under the protection of the Immaculate Heart of Mary.

Father Jean-Paul Bourret, 1923-1983. A Montreal priest on fire, who loved the Scriptures and organized many pilgrimages to Our Lady's shrines, giving weekly talks about her on the radio.

Ernest Gauthier, O.M.I., 1908-1983. Born in North Dakota, Brother Ernest took as his models Brother Anthony Kowalczyk, O.M.I. and Brother André, Founder of St. Joseph's Oratory in Montreal. For his great services he was called "Brother Church." Possessed of a deep desire to become a saint, he had a fervent devotion to Our Lady and loved the priesthood.

Huguette Asselin, 1937-1986, Lévis, Quebec. A member of Opus Dei, she devoted herself to the care of young people, with the help of Our Lady.

Father Eusèbe-Marie Ménard, 1916-1987. Founder of the Holy Apostles Society.

Father Jean-Paul Régimbal, Trinitarian, 1931-1988. Founder of the charismatic movement in Quebec. He said, "Marian Spirituality is summarized in three words: *Ecce*, that is, here am I; *Fiat*, that is, yes to God, do unto me as you will; and *Magnificat*, Mary leads us to joy."

Brother Jacques Burelle, S.G., 1913-1996. This Brother of Saint Gabriel was a teacher in Montreal. During the last 24 years of his life, he was given the task of spreading devotion to Our Lady. He founded the Confraternity of the Rosary and organized musical programs to honour her. To people in trouble he said, "Say your rosary for 15 days to obtain relief and then for 15 days in gratitude." He organized the March of Forgiveness, Marian trains, and numerous pilgrimages.

Our Lady of Combermere
Questing Madonna of The New World

Within sight of the Madawaska River, in a mere crossroads village lost in the vastness of rural Ontario, stands the weathered life-size bronze statue of Our Lady of Combermere near a grove of red pines close to the road. Frequently we associate Marian shrines with the miraculous or extraordinary. In the case of Our Lady of Combermere, who is the patroness of the Madonna House Apostolate, the events leading to her arrival were quite ordinary and unremarkable. This is the essence of Our Lady of Combermere, for she reveals herself as deeply present in the simple aspects of our day-to-day lives. Her miracles are humble and hidden, for she is the tender Mother of lowly, little people the world over, welcoming and embracing them with the open arms of love.

After Catherine Doherty had settled in Combermere in May, 1947, she found herself praying to Our Lady of Combermere in a simple, childlike way, turning to her in her everyday tasks:

"In Russia, where I grew up, and in many other parts of Europe, women are apt to call on Our Lady by the name of their village, county, river, or by any name they use all the time. So in our early days here in Combermere, I began to invoke her under the title of Our Lady of Combermere.

"When I set the bread before I went to Mass in the morning, around 5 a.m., I would say, 'Our Lady of Combermere, watch over this bread and make it rise.' I would talk to her several times a day. When planting seeds I would ask her blessing on them. Looking after the chickens, I asked her to make them lay more eggs and bigger ones. If I went travelling, or nursing, I would ask her to protect me... Such little prayers are so normal that anyone would understand them. Was this not what I had learned as a child in Russia?"

Of great signficance in the growth of devotion to Our Lady of Combermere was the consecration made by Catherine and her husband, Eddie Doherty, in 1951, when they consecrated themselves to Jesus through Mary according to the teachings of St. Louis de Montfort. Catherine called this the beginning of her "journey inward". It brought with it a deeper clarity of vision and firmness of purpose, setting a seal on both her devotion to Our Lady of Combermere and her lay apostolate.

"As time went on," Catherine explains, "things began to happen. There was nothing spectacular or extraordinary in them. At first we didn't notice what was going on. It was only when began to look back that we realized one event followed another and another... On the occasion of the blessing of the chapel in Madonna House on December 8, 1953, Father Cullinane brought us a song to Our Lady of Combermere. The music had been composed by a priest friend of his. We adopted that song, made it our hymn and have sung it ever since."

It was Father Eugene Cullinane, too, who composed a prayer to Our Lady of Combermere. Eventually Bishop Smith, the ordinary of the diocese, graciously granted Madonna House permission to erect a statue of Mary under the title of Our Lady of Combermere and to have it blessed, as well as permission to cast medals in her honour.

The particular image Catherine had in her mind of Our Lady of Combermere became visible in the magnificent bronze statue of her designed and sculpted by Frances Rich, a well-known artist from California. Catherine saw Our Lady as a questing Madonna, a mother rushing to help her children. Her arms are wide open to embrace us. Her face is tender, loving, and a little anxious. She hastens to find us and comfort us.

This statue arrived in Combermere on April 26, 1960, the feast of Our Lady of Good Counsel. It was erected on May 17, and on June 8, now the feast day of Our Lady of Combermere, it was blessed by Bishop Smith with these prophetic words:

"This afternoon in this very blessed part of the diocese, in this very beautiful part of the world, in this month of June, I know that, as the years go by, great graces will flow out all over this diocese, all over Canada and the United States, and all over the rest of the world through Our Lady of Combermere and the great work to which these people have dedicated their lives.

"In blessing the statue of Our Lady of Combermere I have in mind the thought that a great deal of the work necessary to bring the world to the feet of Our Lady will depend on the loyalty and devotion of the friends of Combermere. There has been much progress here. The hand of God is in it. We hope that God will continue, through the hands of Our Blessed Mother, the dispenser of all graces, to bless this hallowed spot.

"We seem to be living in a confused world, one becoming more confused all the time. As the years go by, it seems to me that the solution to the things troubling us will be cared for by Our Lady. She promised to help us, so long as we do our part. So if we listen to her words, in whatever work we do, and dedicate ourselves to her, we will have an opportunity to make recompense to God for many of the sins of the world.

"Now we bless and dedicate the diocese, the country, and all the Americas to Our Lady of Combermere. Graces will go out in abundance from Our Lady of Combermere and we shall all benefit from this center of the lay apostolate, all of us, we in the diocese and those outside."

Through Catherine's reliance on the intercession of Our Lady of Combermere, she found the courage to persevere in her apostolate to the poor and needy, as Madonna House grew into a training centre for the laity, with more than 20 mission houses around the world.

One of the great desires of Catherine's heart was that all men and women everywhere would come to a deep and trusting belief in the love of the Mother of God. She came to realize that more than ever the human race, at this time in its history, needed a mother, the most powerful and loving Mother of God, Our Lady of Combermere. Catherine also saw how eager our Mother was to assist us, to heal us, to guide us in every way.

Most people in the world are called to live the hidden life of Jesus, Mary and Joseph in Nazareth. When we open our hearts to the presence of the Holy Spirit, our seemingly uneventful lives become as extraordinary as those of the Holy Family. This is why we call on Our Lady. She is the spouse of the Holy Spirit. When she is present, the Holy Spirit overshadows us too. What we thought of as boring or menial work is transformed into incarnate love. Whatever burdens we are carrying are lifted from us and put into the heart of Christ.

Today our secular society places many pressures on those striving to be faithful to the Gospel. All around us moral law is being rejected. It seems perfectly normal to please myself, to do what I want. We struggle mightily with our own weaknesses. We can become very discouraged by the darkness around us. This is why our good God has sent us his Mother. She knows how to enter this wilderness of the present age and sustain her children who struggle in it. When we pray to Our Lady of Combermere she hears the cries of our hearts and intercedes for us, covering us with her mantle.

In this prayer Catherine captures the essential qualities of this Questing Madonna of the New World:

"Beloved Mary, Our Lady of Combermere, you are the Mother of all men and women, for your Son has made you so. When he was dying on the cross he gave you to Saint John, and he gave Saint John to you. In one gesture he who was not able to make any gestures, because he was crucified, made you the Mother of everyone. We are all your children. Unseen, you bend down tenderly over each one of us. If we would only pause for a minute, if we would only quiet our poor minds and enter your great silence, we would know how lovingly you hold us in your arms.

"In these days so many of your children are fragmented; so many wish to die; so many do not know where they are going; so many are refugees, lost in the immense deserts of our huge cities.

"Take pity on us. Take pity on us because we are the most pitiful people ever. You see us—Catholics, Orthodox, Protestants, Jews, Moslems, Buddhists, Hindus, peoples of all religions. You see every one of us and, whereas the arms of your Son were crucified, yours are outstretched to embrace the whole world. Your arms are ready to hold any of us who come to you, and you long to sing us a lullaby. You are always a Mother. That is what you have been created for—to be the Mother of God and of all people.

"So we come to you, first bowing low before the Father, the Son and the Holy Spirit, making upon ourselves the sign of the Holy Cross. In this we find our healing.

"Beloved Mother, take me into your arms. Hold me tight. Give me strength for another day. Amen."

Also by Fr. Émile-Marie Brière

The Power of Love
I Met the Humbled Christ in Russia

by Catherine de Hueck Doherty

Bogoroditza: She Who Gave Birth to God
Dear Father
Fragments of My Life
The Gospel Without Compromise
Molchanie
My Russian Yesterdays
Not Without Parables
Poustinia
Sobornost
Strannik
Urodivoi

by Eddie Doherty

A Cricket in My Heart
Gall and Honey

These and other titles are available through
Madonna House Publications
Combermere, Ontario, Canada K0J 1L0
(613) 756-3728
www.madonnahouse.org

MADONNA HOUSE PUBLICATIONS
Combermere • Ontario • Canada • K0J 1L0

The aim of our publications is to share the Gospel of Jesus Christ with all people from all walks of life.

It is to awaken and deepen in our readers an experience of God's love in the most simple and ordinary facets of everyday life.

It is to make known to our readers how to live the tender, saving life of God in everything they do and for everyone they meet.

Our publications are dedicated to Our Lady of Combermere, the Mother of Jesus and of His Church, and we are under her protection and care.

Madonna House Publications is a non-profit apostolate of Madonna House within the Catholic Church. Donations allow us to send books to people who cannot afford them but most need them all around the world. Thank you for your participation in this apostolate.

To request a catalogue of our current publications, please call (613) 756-3728, or write to us at:

>Madonna House Publications
>2888 Dafoe Rd
>Combermere ON   K0J 1L0
>Canada

You can also visit us on the Internet at the following address:

>www.madonnahouse.org